# THE EVERYTHING® GUIDE TO BEING A REAL ESTATE AGENT

Dear Reader,
When I was asked to author this book, I found it to be a challenge. Every skilled real estate agent has her own ideas about what it takes to be a good agent, and I am no exception. Nearly two decades in the business have helped me develop my own style and manner of doing business. The purpose of this book, though, is to give you the information you need to be the best real estate agent *you* can be. While my real estate experience is very helpful, working on this book has caused me to question and investigate what I know. I was duty bound to examine my opinions and methods, so I researched the many topics covered here and made every attempt to include information from varying viewpoints.

The effort has given me a fresh perspective and I believe it has made me a better real estate agent. The advantage for you is that you have a book written by a practicing, experienced agent with a broad scope and an open mind. I believe it will make you a better agent as well.

I have loved being a real estate agent from the day I started my career in 1988 and nothing has changed that fact for me. My hope for you is that you will find the same love for real estate and that you will also find the direction you need to help you in your new and exciting career.

Shahri Masters

# THE EVERYTHING® GUIDE TO BEING A REAL ESTATE AGENT

Secrets to a successful career!

Shahri Masters

Adams Media
Avon, Massachusetts

## *Dedication*

*This book is dedicated to the real estate agent who gave me my earliest memories of what it means to have this career, who talked to me about real estate from before the day I was born until he passed away, months before my tenth birthday, my grandfather, Albert Edward Norman.*

• • •

Publishing Director: Gary M. Krebs
Director of Product Development: Paula Munier
Associate Managing Editor: Laura M. Daly
Associate Copy Chief: Brett Palana-Shanahan
Acquisitions Editor: Kate Burgo
Development Editor: Rachel Engelson
Associate Production Editor: Casey Ebert
Director of Manufacturing: Susan Beale
Associate Director of Production: Michelle Roy Kelly
Cover Design: Paul Beatrice, Erick DaCosta Matt LeBlanc
Layout and Graphics: Colleen Cunningham, Holly Curtis, Sorae Lee



Published by Adams Media, an F+W Publications Company
57 Littlefield Street, Avon, MA 02322 U.S.A.
*www.adamsmedia.com*

ISBN 10: 1-59337-432-1
ISBN 13: 978-1-59337-432-7

Printed in the United States of America.

J I H G F E D C B

**Library of Congress Cataloging-in-Publication Data**
Masters, Shahri.
The everything guide to being a real estate agent : secrets to a successful career! / Shahri Masters.
p. cm.
ISBN 1-59337-432-1
1. Real estate agents--United States. 2. Real estate business--Vocational guidance--United States. I. Title: Guide to being a real estate agent. II. Title.

HD278.M37 2006
333.33068--dc22

2005033326

## *Acknowledgments*

Thank you.

To my husband David, who loves me, supports me, and takes care of me so that I have the ability to be a real estate agent and an author.

To my daughter Abby, who loves me and understands, better than any child, what it means to be a grownup.

To all the real estate agents who have been an example, teaching me through their words and actions how to be better at my craft.

And to my clients and customers, who have let me "practice" on them, learning with each transaction how to excel in real estate.

• • •

# Contents

# Top Ten Things You'll Learn in This Book

1. Discover your motivation for becoming a real estate agent and learn about the nuts and bolts of the business.
2. Learn how goal setting provides the structure that will bring you success.
3. Effective time management is essential to your job satisfaction and achievement in real estate.
4. Learn to read and understand your clients and customers, to better guide them through the process of buying and selling real estate.
5. How to recognize and cultivate your sphere of influence.
6. Learn to prospect for business and market your services.
7. The ins and outs of guiding your sellers, preparing properties for sale, and pricing and marketing your listings.
8. Discern a buyer's needs, discover their hopes, find the right property, and write the offer.
9. Learn what to expect and how to prepare for your new career.
10. Find out if opening your own office is the next step for you.

# Introduction

Welcome to *The Everything® Guide to Being a Real Estate Agent.* Perhaps you are reading this book to research a new career path and wonder if real estate is the right choice for you. You may have already decided that you want to be a real estate agent and are looking for some direction in your career choice. Maybe you are an agent already and want to find some pointers to help you become a better agent. No matter which category you fall into, there is something in this book for you.

If you are still making a decision about your career path and real estate is one of the opportunities you are exploring, you will learn about the education requirements and the ongoing training. You will get a realistic picture of the job description of a real estate agent and you will learn what types of financial commitments you will need to make.

If you have already decided to become a real estate agent and are looking for direction in your new career, you will learn the basics for getting started, getting organized, setting goals, and working with other professionals. You will learn the benefits of specialization, of working with a team, and of working alone. You will learn about your sphere of influence and client record keeping.

If you have been an agent for a while and want to get to the next level of success in your career, you will get instructions for more effectively working with your buyers and sellers. You will learn how to perfect your people skills and how to better market the properties you represent. You will also have the chance to decide if opening your own office is the direction you want to pursue.

You will all discover how the World Wide Web can help your career. You will get a handle on time management, learn the pitfalls to avoid, and receive the tools necessary to take your career to the next level.

Pursuing a career in real estate can be very demanding. In this book you will learn how to balance your real estate life with your personal life. You will learn who to turn to for help when things are tough or when you are ready to expand your business.

Real estate can be a very lucrative career. It can also be very rewarding. People tend to associate property ownership with security. As a real estate agent, you are in a position to help people achieve a level of security and also to realize important personal and financial ambitions. You may help them find their first home or their dream home, their first office for a new business, or their new corporate headquarters. Whether they want to own their own home or advance their financial standing by purchasing a second home or other rental property, you can help people reach their goals. You will play a significant role that results in happy clients and job satisfaction for the dedicated agent.

This book will arm you with important information to help you embark on your exciting career with direction and confidence.

Chapter 1

# So You Want to Be a Real Estate Agent

**People choose to** pursue a career in real estate for many reasons. Some enjoy working with the public. Some feel it's a career that will let them control their own schedules. Some have heard the pay is good, maybe even lucrative. Many are interested in buying real estate themselves and think that agents always have the inside track to "the best deals." Regardless of your motivation, it's important to know the realities of working as a real estate agent before you decide to get your license.

## *A Full-Time Career*

Talk to the people who are enrolled in real estate prelicensing schools and you'll find that many of them think they can be successful real estate agents by keeping their current jobs and working real estate part-time. While that is possible, it's not likely. Developing a successful career as a real estate agent takes a great deal of time and effort, more than what is typically available when working a part-time schedule.

**Essential**

Interview real estate agents in and outside of your community. Ask them what they like and what they don't like about the business. Ask them their motivations for starting in the real estate business and if their motivations have changed.

It's true that cell phones and e-mail make communicating with potential buyers and sellers easier. However, the public recognizes the real estate office as the place to go for real estate help. A part-time agent who operates out of a distant location is not as likely to encounter the same number of potential new clients and customers as he would while working at the real estate office.

Successful real estate agents treat their jobs as they would any other full-time position. They are at the office at least five days a week, often six, and sometimes seven. They come and go as they work with buyers and sellers but the office is their home base, the place where people who want to buy and sell real estate can find them.

## *Working with the Public*

When you interview agents about why they are in real estate they will often say, "I'm a people person." Having a good understanding of people can help you succeed in sales, as it can help you succeed in virtually any endeavor. Working with the public can be rewarding but it can also be trying. Realize that people are going to have their good days and their bad days. There will be times when they take out their bad days on you. Patience and understanding on your part will keep you from getting your feelings hurt while learning how to handle each situation.

You will work with people through what is often a stressful time. You will be helping them to make a correct decision about one of the greatest financial investments of their lives. They can get scared, angry, frustrated, and worried—often all at the same time! Being able to flow with the changes, as they go through the highs and lows of purchasing or selling (and sometimes both), will keep your stress level lower and easier to manage.

## *Finding Your First Sales*

Did you know that the bulk of an established real estate agent's income is earned by working with past clients who are ready to buy or sell again and from new people who those past clients send to the agent as referrals? A good agent's referral base grows each year, contributing more and more to her income.

A new real estate agent comes into the business cold, without a backlog of returning clients. Sure, you might have family and friends who are planning to buy or sell real estate, but how many, and how often will they buy? You must have an ongoing source of clients to be successful over the long term. The only way to build your client base is to work the job aggressively.

### Fact

New agents usually have an easier time finding buyers than sellers. The main reason is that sellers have been previous buyers and may already know an agent they trust. It makes sense for new agents to spend their first weeks finding as many potential buyers as possible.

To improve your chances of finding business quickly, make sure your family members, friends, and acquaintances know you are in real estate and can help them buy or sell. Also, train them to tell their friends about you. Wear a name badge that identifies you as a real estate agent. You'll be surprised how many people stop you in the grocery store or post office to ask about local properties. Join civic clubs and other organizations where you'll meet new people. Volunteer at a local charity thrift shop or other busy location. In short, make yourself visible.

As you gain recognition as a real estate agent, you will begin to develop a reputation by answering questions. Most people are curious about real estate. They like to know what has sold in their area and the price of their neighbor's house. You will be asked questions about financing and whether or not it is appropriate to remodel. To become a valuable source of information, learn everything you can about your market. Once you are known as someone who has the answers, you will become the choice for people who need a real estate agent.

## Becoming Familiar with Agent Resources

You can't help buyers find a property until you know your market and have a good understanding of the search tools available to you. Spend a portion of each day getting accustomed to your Multiple

Listing Service's system (MLS). An MLS is an organization that's formed for the purpose of sharing listings, which you'll likely find to be Internet based. Print information about current and sold listings and drive by the properties. Preview the interiors if possible, paying close attention to differences in home styles and neighborhoods. Pay particular attention to areas of town that are unfamiliar to you, so that when a buyer asks you a question you can answer with confidence.

If agents in your area are responsible for writing offers, spend time becoming familiar with the forms that are used. Get to know affiliated real estate professionals, such as appraisers, home and pest inspectors, attorneys, and surveyors.

**Essential**

Read the *offer and acceptance* form, as well as the other forms that are used in your state. Be sure that you understand the boilerplate version, and learn what belongs in each blank on the form. Practice writing offers and have a seasoned agent, or your broker, review them for you.

With all of that to accomplish, you might wonder when you'll have time to be at the office—but don't worry, you will. As a matter of fact, many things can be done at the office, such as learning the forms and researching the MLS. Just hanging around the office and listening in on the conversations of more experienced agents can offer insight and tell you more of what you need to know. Don't expect to learn everything in one day, or two weeks, or even in a month. Learning your market and finding buyers is an ongoing process, one you'll get better at as you gain experience.

## Controlling Your Schedule

Some new agents have a difficult time organizing their days. This is especially true for those who have always worked a nine-to-five job, where someone else told them how to spend their time. Now that their schedules are up to them, they are lost. Once you recognize that time management is important, it's easy to make your schedule work for you.

Make daily to-do lists and prioritize them; force yourself to complete every item on your list by the end of each day. There will be times when you can't possibly complete all of the tasks you have set for yourself, but, if you do them in order of priority, you will get to the most important tasks. Completing these daily tasks will give you a sense of accomplishment, boost your morale, and help preserve your motivation to start the next day with a fresh set of goals. (We'll talk more about time management in Chapter 5.)

Some goals involve tasks that can't be accomplished in one day. Record these long-term goals on a separate list and refer to them daily to make sure you are on track to their completion. (There is more about goal setting in Chapter 4.)

Arrange your schedule carefully. Allow plenty of time to work on your to-do list and your list of goals. At the end of thirty days, go back and review your accomplishments. Did you meet your own expectations? If not, why? Analyze the way you used your time to determine if changes to your schedule will help you work more effectively.

## *Great Pay?*

Wanting to make a good income is a great motivator for getting into the real estate business, and the potential is there to actually become wealthy. Being realistic about how much you can make, and how quickly, is also important. From real estate school to your license, to business cards and marketing materials—it is essential that you are aware that you will be writing a lot of checks before you receive one. Be prepared for this. (We'll talk more about managing your finances in Chapter 15.)

You may spend hours and hours with someone who never buys or sells and you could also have the good fortune of spending very little time with someone and receiving a sizable commission. You cannot predict how these things will go and having unrealistic expectations can set you up for disappointment.

### The Client's Best Interest

If you are only in real estate for the money, it stands to reason that you will not always be working in your clients' or customers' best interest. Having money as your primary goal will direct your efforts toward your own best interest, often to your clients' detriment. Your clients will realize this and, even if they complete a transaction with you, they will not refer you to their friends and family. Without referrals, your business will eventually fold. However, if your clients' and customers' best interests are your first priority, they will refer their friends and family to you and you will make good money. Success will come from focusing on the service you provide, instead of the income.

**E Alert**

Most states do not allow you to pay a referral fee, or kickback, to anyone except licensed real estate agents and attorneys. Thanking people for referrals is important, but *paying* for referrals can lose you your license! Taking a friend to lunch is usually just fine; be creative *and legal* in how you reward referrals.

### Being Self-Employed

If you've always worked as an employee, you are accustomed to being on the job during specific hours, on specific days, as dictated by your employer. No matter how your days are spent, you receive a paycheck for your time. Your employer also deducts taxes from each paycheck and sends tax payments to governmental agencies. When you file your taxes, a refund is often forthcoming.

**Essential**

A small percentage of real estate agents are employees of their firms. Although an employee arrangement is not typical in the real estate world, it is something you should clarify when interviewing for a position.

Working in real estate is very different. You're in charge of your own schedule and put in as many or as few hours as you choose.

At first, your pay may seem to have absolutely nothing to do with the number of hours you work. You may put in hundreds of hours before you receive a paycheck (called a commission check), and it may account for only some of the hours you actually spent working. You may have other instances where you spend very little time and receive compensation that far exceeds the hours expended. When you do get that first commission check, you'll see that it's a lump sum with no tax deductions. It's up to you to pay any taxes owed to your state or the federal government.

Most licensed real estate agents are considered statutory nonemployees by the IRS, and are treated as self-employed individuals if a few conditions are met.

1. Payments for their services as real estate agents are the direct result of sales or other efforts, and are not related to the number of hours they worked.
2. The firm and agent have entered into a written contract that stipulates the agent will not be treated as an employee for federal tax purposes.

Agents are often asked to do "floor duty." This entails working in the office for a certain number of hours or days each month, answering phone calls and helping customers who walk in unannounced. An agent is also expected to adhere to a firm's formal policies and procedures and might be expected to produce a certain amount of business for the company in order to continue working there. Even though the real estate firm controls your time and performance to some extent, neither of those requirements makes an agent an employee if the two IRS rules are met.

### Fact

You may hear the term *independent contractor* used to describe a self-employed agent. That designation has the same meaning as *statutory nonemployee.*

Real estate agents typically pay estimated taxes on a quarterly basis. The amount they pay is based on the amount they earned during the current quarter or expect to earn during the next. Tax estimates are sometimes difficult for a new agent, whose closings and pay can be sporadic. A tax professional can help you determine how much to pay each quarter, but it's up to you to put aside a portion of each commission check so that the funds are available when the payment comes due.

## Plan to Spend Money

Most real estate transactions take at least thirty days, and often longer, to complete. The best-case scenario would be to make a sale on your very first day as an agent and collect a commission check for it in a month. Unfortunately (unless you have a friend or relative waiting to buy a house from you), first sales don't usually happen that quickly. In most real estate markets, new agents should plan to have enough extra savings to cover at least six months of living expenses—more if possible.

Now that you're self-employed, you'll have to pay for your own health insurance, an expense your employer might have contributed to in the past. Your auto insurance will go up as soon as you begin using your vehicle for business purposes. You'll also need a cell phone with plenty of available minutes. Some agents like to use a pager too. You will have plenty of other start-up expenses, including:

- Prelicensing school costs
- Licensing exam fee
- Required business licensing
- Fees to join a local Multiple Listing Service (MLS)
- Fees to join a local Board of Realtors® (usually in conjunction with the MLS)
- Ongoing fees for local real estate organizations
- Expenses of doing business, which vary depending on the agency you choose
- Errors and omissions insurance coverage
- Business cards and promotional materials

Plan ahead for these expenses and be sure to prepare your significant other for your dip in income and possible long working hours.

## *Only Handling Your Own Deals*

Do you want to be a real estate agent simply to handle your own real estate transactions? Take the prelicensing class to learn about your local real estate laws and customs, but delay getting your license until you are sure it's the best solution for your needs. There are pros and cons associated with being licensed if you do not plan to work it as a career.

Agents must always disclose that they are licensed agents when dealing with the public, and that includes for sale by owner sellers. Have you seen real estate classifieds that say "no agents"? They're fairly common. Disclosing your agent status to a seller who has already made the decision to sell the property on his own is often an immediate turnoff. They sometimes won't even talk with you.

Real estate agents are governed by a state licensing board and they are expected to adhere to and stay well informed about local and federal real estate laws. That doesn't mean you can neglect the law if you remain unlicensed, but if you become an agent and make an error during the transaction, you are subject to reprimand and discipline by your state licensing board.

**E Alert**

Agents have greater liability when buying and selling property for themselves than the general public has. Not only can a mistake cost you your license, but you may also be sued and the mistake could cost you considerable money, time, and headaches.

Agents do have early knowledge of new listings and they are in the right place to learn about properties before they even go on the market. An agent's ongoing experience gives her valuable insight into the local real estate market, making it easier to recognize when a property is truly a good buy.

## It's Not about Sales

Successful real estate agents don't "sell" real estate. They help people find and acquire properties they love. There's a big difference between those two concepts that everyone who has shown property understands: hard-sale tactics don't work with most real estate buyers. You don't have to sell them on something. They know exactly whether or not they like a property, often the minute they see it.

Being a real estate agent is a bit like being a combination counselor, detective, and coordination expert:

- **A counselor**—because you must listen carefully to what clients say and watch their actions to determine their wants and needs
- **A detective**—because it takes intuition and excellent search skills to find just the right property
- **A coordination expert**—to make sure everyone is doing what is required to get to closing

These attributes are a part of true sales ability. In the same way as showing property or creating marketing materials, these skills will become second nature as you learn and practice them.

## Your Image

Whether you live in a metropolitan area or a rural area, a suburb or a resort, your image must reflect the styles and needs of your community. This does not mean your image must be a sham. Even the most naive person can spot a phony image. It does mean that you may need to adjust how you present yourself, to best be received by the public.

Appropriate dress in a metropolitan area may be a business suit, but if you are selling ranch lands, you can probably wear jeans and boots. In a resort, you can be more casual but cautiously so. If you are just a bit *less* casual than your customers, you will be regarded as the professional.

A good, clean, working car is essential. In order to allow your clients comfortable access to the back seat, a four-door automobile is optimal. Keep your car free of junk. You should not be moving papers or yesterday's jacket before someone can get into your vehicle. If your car is older and unpredictable, but you cannot afford to replace it at this time, take it to a reputable mechanic and pay for a complete service. Be sure the tires, brakes, transmission, and engine are in perfect running order. Take your car in for regular service to minimize the risk of breaking down.

### Essential

The exterior of the car should also be well kept. Broken taillights or unattended dents are not part of the image you want to portray. A good wax job can make an older car sparkle.

You don't need to be an experienced salesperson to succeed in real estate. You do need to be a person who is committed to working with your clients and customers—from the first hellos to sitting with them at the closing table.

Chapter 2

# Education and Licensing

**You'll be prepared** to tackle your prelicensing class and state exam with enthusiasm if you take some time to learn the facts about what it takes to become a real estate agent in your state. Licensing tests are tough, but knowing what to expect keeps your stress level down as you move through the prelicensing period.

## *State Licensing Laws*

Each state in the United States determines its own real estate licensing requirements. If you did a national study, you would find that the steps you must take to become an agent vary quite a bit from state to state. Be sure to get the facts about licensing requirements in your state before you decide to become a real estate agent.

Some states require that you complete a certain number of college credits before you can become a licensed real estate agent. However, in most areas, you can become a licensed salesperson by attending specialized classes and passing an exam that proves you understand the topics that were covered.

The length of class time required before taking your test varies widely, but sixty to seventy-five hours seems to be average for those seeking a salesperson's license. Plan on additional classes for broker licensing.

Some states allow you to become licensed before you have made arrangements to work for a real estate firm. Others require that a broker-in-charge of a firm sponsor you before you can take the exam, or before your license is issued.

Most states have two main types of class requirements: a general real estate knowledge course and a course in real estate law, applicable to the individual state. Some states test these two requirements separately, so that if you pass one test but not the other, you do not have to take both exams again.

### Fact

Real estate brokers are allowed to work without supervision, but sales agents must always be supervised by a licensed broker. Some states do not allow you to become a broker until you've had a specific amount of sales experience, while others prefer that you become a broker from the very beginning.

### Your Background

License application forms nearly always contain questions about your character. Have you been convicted of any type of crime? Do you have traffic violations related to driving under the influence of drugs or alcohol? Don't be tempted to provide false information on your application. If your offense was minor, chances are your application will be approved. However, if the state discovers that you were dishonest, you will very likely lose your license—no matter how many years of experience you obtain before the discovery.

### Alert

Dishonest agents have stolen deposit funds and steered clients into questionable transactions and loans, so states are justifiably cautious about allowing someone with a criminal record to work in real estate. States try to ensure that professionals who are entrusted with helping the public are not likely to intentionally cause harm.

Many states no longer rely on the word of the applicant; they require you to submit a police report along with your application. You may have to submit to fingerprinting or a background check. Your state real estate commission can tell you exactly what is required and how to obtain the necessary documents.

Each state has a real estate authority, which governs real estate transactions and administers the state's specific requirements and regulations. They are usually called the Real Estate Commission or Real Estate Division. In addition to getting in touch with your state real estate commission to obtain documents, you may call them for information about education guidelines or rules and regulations that may affect you. Note that the Real Estate Commission or Real Estate Division cannot give you legal advice but can direct you to the resources you need to learn what is required.

Your license application might also ask if you've declared bankruptcy, had a loan that was foreclosed, or been issued a judgment for nonpayment of a debt or back child support, even if a judgment has not been issued. Answer the questions honestly. If you are concerned that your application will be rejected for any reason, call your licensing commission and ask for an explanation of its general guidelines for applicant background requirements.

### Finding Your State Licensing Agency

All state licensing commissions have Web sites, but some offer more online help than others. The most complete Web sites offer information for current agents, prospective agents, and the general public.

It's easy to find state agency Web sites. Go to one of the major search engines, such as Google located at *www.google.com*. Search for the term *real estate commission*, adding your state name or abbreviation after those words—such as, *real estate commission fl*, to search for Florida information. That type of search usually locates state agencies, even those that use other words in their official names.

Local real estate firms can also provide contact information. See Appendix C for more information about locating your state real estate commission.

### Becoming Licensed in Multiple States

Some states offer reciprocal licensing, which means that if you are licensed in state A, you can bypass some of the requirements to be licensed in state B. You might be allowed to skip licensing classes and go straight to the testing phase. In some cases, you can even bypass the test and simply pay a fee to be licensed in the new state. Many states require that you take the state law portion of the class and pass a state law exam. Don't assume reciprocity. Check to see how the laws apply.

Commercial real estate agents often deal with clients and sales in many states, so multiple licenses can be a plus. Agents who specialize in residential sales usually focus on their local area, making extra licenses less critical unless they work in towns where sales overlap state lines.

## Prelicensing Schools

The prelicensing school you choose must be approved by your state to provide real estate education, otherwise you won't be allowed to take your state exam. Residents of larger cities can often choose from multiple schools, but if you live in a small town or rural area, you might have to drive a bit to find even one school.

The brokers-in-charge at local real estate firms are a good source for information about prelicensing schools. They generally know which schools are the best and can provide you with contact information. Ask agents for their opinions as well. New agents are a particularly good source, because their school experience is still fresh in their minds.

### Fact

A real estate broker is someone who has passed an advanced exam that shows he or she is capable of working with no supervision. A firm's broker-in-charge is a broker who is responsible for trust funds and must supervise the firm's agents and employees to make sure they abide by local real estate laws.

Many community colleges offer prelicensing classes at an affordable price. They are usually semester-long classes held in conjunction with other community education offerings. They are a good choice for people who want a little more time to become familiar with real estate facts before taking a licensing exam.

### Class Options

Schools that specialize in real estate education usually offer daytime and evening classes that are held either once or twice each week, running for the total number of hours required by the state. So, a sixty-hour class that requires you to attend six hours each week would take ten weeks to complete. Keep in mind that most states have strict guidelines about missed classes. If you have too many absences, you'll have to retake the class.

Some schools offer cram classes, often conducted in long sessions during two or more weekends. That type of instruction is best used as a refresher course for someone who already understands the basics of local real estate law.

Some states allow you to take your prelicensing class online or by correspondence. Check your state laws to find out if that is possible where you live.

**Essential**

> Prelicensing school teaches you real estate facts, which are essential, but they are not always topics that guarantee you'll stay awake during class. Finding a teacher who knows how to combine facts with a bit of storytelling is a great way to ensure you'll remember the things you need to know at test time.

Your state real estate commission has a list of approved schools located throughout your state. Visit their Web site or give them a call if you want to gather information about all prelicensing opportunities before you make a decision.

### Opting for a College Degree

Many colleges and universities offer degrees related to real estate. Some are graduate programs that you can pursue after receiving an undergraduate business degree. Others are undergraduate programs with an emphasis on real estate and related fields.

## Broker or Agent: Which Is Best for You?

Whether you want to become a broker or an agent depends on the time (and money) you have for education and the way you want to use your license. Brokers can work on their own, with no supervision, while salespeople cannot; the broker-in-charge at a real estate firm must supervise them. Weigh the pros and cons to determine which path you should take.

Some states do not allow you to be a broker without apprenticing under another broker for a period of time, usually about two years. Even if you get a broker's license, you may not be allowed to work without supervision for a while.

There are plenty of real estate agents who have every bit as much experience as a broker, but no interest in acquiring the title. Sales is their passion and they don't plan to own their own real estate firms. A broker-in-charge of a firm supervises salespeople, but other brokers affiliated with the firm must still abide by office policies and procedures. In other words, the type of license you hold doesn't always affect the way you work for an agency.

Some firms now require all of their agents to be brokers because brokers have proven that they have more knowledge of real estate. Their advanced standing means they shoulder more responsibility for their own actions than a supervised salesperson does. That results in fewer problems for the firm if someone files a formal complaint against a broker.

### E Alert

All conscientious firms carry errors and omissions insurance, which is a type of malpractice insurance for real estate agencies and agents. Commonly referred to as *E&O insurance*, the rates are typically lower for firms that are staffed entirely by brokers than they are for agencies that use sales agents.

Acquiring a broker's license pushes you to learn more about the business of real estate. If you need that push to follow through with your education, preparing for the test will certainly provide it. Get accustomed to the idea of becoming a broker. It is likely that many states will eventually require every agent to have a broker's license to help ensure that they are qualified to help the public buy and sell real estate.

## Test-Taking Tips

It's normal for prospective agents to be nervous about the exam that is required to obtain a real estate salesperson or broker license. After all, most of them are adults who have been in another career for a while and they haven't taken a test for a long time. Yes, the tests are usually difficult, but you'll ease the exam stress by being prepared.

### Question

**What happens if I fail my exam?**

Most states let you retake the real estate exam if you fail it the first time. Check your state laws to find out how many times you are allowed to take the exam before you must re-enroll in prelicensing school.

The number one aspect of the test that most potential real estate agents or brokers are afraid of is the real estate math portion. You can feel better about tackling this part of the exam if you pay close attention during classes so that you understand the mathematical formulas that are used most often by real estate agents. The majority of them are simple and focus on calculations you'll eventually make for your clients, such as how much a house must sell for in order for the seller to have X amount of money left over at closing. Most states allow you to bring a calculator to the exam. You still need to know the formula, but you can plug it in to the calculator to get your answer.

Some math problems will involve the HUD-1, which is the standard real estate closing statement that identifies all funds associated with a transaction. Broker tests usually include more closing-statement questions than salesperson exams, but everyone should be prepared for them.

If you don't feel comfortable with the math, purchase a real estate math handbook and work the problems as many times as it takes for you to grasp them. Prelicensing schools usually sell their favorite math books.

### Find Sample Tests

Your school probably sells workbooks or computer software filled with sample tests that are similar to the real estate exams given in your state. You'll also find sample tests online, but make sure they are designed specifically for the state where you will take your test. None of the samples will be an exact match to a state exam, but using them for practice tests will reveal your strengths and weaknesses. Don't wait too long to start practicing. You'll need time to strengthen your skills if you score low on some topics.

**E Alert**

You must pass a test administered by your school before you are allowed to take the state exam. The test might be very similar to a state test, or it might not. If you breeze through your school's test, don't assume the state exam will be easy. Keep studying and practicing until you are comfortable with all of the subjects.

### The Night Before

Read over your notes but don't stay up all hours cramming facts into your head. If you don't know the information the day before the test, one more night won't be much help. Lay out everything you need for test day—from the clothes you plan to wear to the identification testers will require. Get a good night's sleep and make sure to set your alarm. You might be too nervous to eat a large meal right before the test, but try to eat something that morning so that your blood sugar remains stable. Avoid caffeinated beverages if they tend to make you jittery; you want the calmest nerves possible during your test! Don't forget to leave early, in case you run into a traffic snarl.

### During the Test

The staff at your prelicensing school probably explained the grading procedures. If all of the questions are worth the same amount of points, don't spend time obsessing over any one of them. If you don't know an answer, move on. You can come back to the question later and perhaps one of the questions ahead will trigger your memory.

Read each question carefully. It's not unusual for the questions to contain a phrase or word that sounds like a fact you've heard over and over, but has a very different meaning in the context of the question. Pace yourself and move carefully from question to question. During the exam, try to remain calm and remember: It's only a test. If your first attempt isn't successful, you'll know what to expect the second time.

## *Ongoing Education and Training*

Once you've made it through prelicensing school and passed your state test, will you know how to be a real estate agent? For most new agents, the answer is no. Nothing you've learned so far has prepared you for the actual craft of being an agent, but not to worry. There are plenty of ways to continue your real estate education and training. Using a combination of methods will put you on the path to success.

### Required Continuing Education

When it comes to learning about the real estate business, going to real estate school and passing the exam is just the beginning. Some of the learning will come as on-the-job training and some of it will be in the form of continuing education.

Licensed real estate agents are required to take continuing-education classes that keep them up to date on changes to state real estate laws. The number of hours required by each state varies, and so does the timing of the classes. In some states, agents have a two-year period in which to take the total number of required class hours. Other states demand that you take at least a portion of the classes each year. Check your state's requirements for continuing education when you are looking into the initial requirements for obtaining a license. Your first year in real estate will pass quickly. Don't risk waiting until the last minute to schedule classes. Try to take a class or two every month and collect the hours slowly. This will allow you to absorb more from each class and it will keep you from scrambling to find available classes when it is time to renew your license.

## Essential

Most states allow you to take at least a portion of your continuing education online, at your convenience. Your local prelicensing school can probably help you find a qualifying online class.

Your continuing-education hours might be broken into two parts: a required update that informs you of changes to real estate laws, and additional hours for an elective class that covers a topic of your choice. Extra hours spent in elective classes—over and above what is required—can often be carried over and used to satisfy education requirements for the next reporting period.

Your state might allow new licensees to skip the first year of continuing education, because they've already spent a great deal of time in class and learned current laws in preparation for the licensing exam. Other states require additional education for first-year agents, even more than is required for experienced agents.

Your state real estate commission must approve all continuing-education schools, teachers, and classes. There is a good chance that your prelicensing school also offers continuing education. If you felt the teachers were good, start there when looking for classes. Your local Board of Realtors® will offer information about local continuing-education classes, and so will your state real estate commission.

### Should You Become a Realtor®?

It is common for members of the public to call all real estate agents "Realtor®," but not every agent has the right to use that title.

A Realtor® is a real estate professional who is a member of the National Association of Realtors®, a trade organization that is called the NAR, for short. There are more than 1 million Realtors® in nearly sixty countries worldwide.

The broker or owner of a real estate office generally makes a decision whether or not to join the National Association of Realtors®. If he does, his entire office would need to be members as well. All agents in the office would be required to adhere to the higher code of ethics, their listings would be available in the Realtor® MLS and on *www.realtor.com*, and they would enjoy all the other benefits of membership in NAR. If the office does not choose to affiliate with NAR, all the agents in the office would be nonmembers. This is often the case with developers selling their own subdivisions only, who have no need to access MLS or other National Association of Realtor® services.

**Fact**

*Realtor®* is a federally registered collective membership mark that identifies a real estate professional who is a Member of the National Association of Realtors® and subscribes to its strict Code of Ethics.

## Benefits for Your Realtor® Dues

You must pay annual dues to be a Realtor®, but the NAR offers many benefits to its members that make these dues worth their cost. Following are some of the benefits offered by the NAR to its members:

- A monthly magazine with articles that teach agents to work responsibly and productively, and to promote their businesses
- Access to password-protected educational materials at NAR and state affiliated Web sites
- Representatives who lobby for Realtor® needs and personal property rights, at the local, state, and national levels

- A Realtor® VIP program that offers member discounts for many products and services
- Ongoing education through Realtor University Online® and special designation programs
- Access to a large real estate library filled with books, tapes, and other educational media
- Annual state and national conferences where Realtors® can network with each other and take advantage of educational opportunities
- Having your listings be a part of the Multiple Listing Service (MLS) available online through *www.Realtor.com*

While you may not take advantage of all of these resources, they are available anytime you need them. The educational materials alone are worth the cost of membership.

One important quality that sets Realtors® apart from other agents is their commitment to abide by the Realtor® Code of Ethics, which is a document that details numerous requirements to maintain membership, including an agent's responsibilities of loyalty and legal duties to clients. The ethics document also covers truthfulness in advertising and offers guidelines for working honestly and in harmony with others in the real estate profession.

### E Alert

Your local Board of Realtors® will require that you take specific types of continuing education on a regular basis to remain a member in good standing and will often offer free classes for members.

Realtors® police their own members. Every Realtor® has the power to file a complaint against another Realtor® if necessary, and the organization also accepts complaints from the general public. These complaints can affect membership status and fines can be levied against you if a panel of your peers determines you have acted inappropriately. However, the organization does not have the ability to take away your real estate license. That action can only be taken by the real estate licensing commission that granted the license.

### Special Designation Programs

Your prelicensing class taught you the basics of real estate law in your state, but it probably didn't touch on an essential ingredient to your success: how to be a good real estate agent. There are many special designation programs, each one offering training in a specific topic and all designed to teach you the business of real estate. Membership in the NAR is required for most designations.

The training requirements vary for each designation. Some are available through home study if you meet certain eligibility guidelines, such as a minimum number of years in the business or possession of another designation. Be prepared to pay an annual fee to retain memberships in the groups that award special designations. Continuing education might also be required.

**Essential**

Some of the classes you must take to become accredited for special designations are probably accepted by your state for required continuing education. The trainers at each course can tell you which portions are approved by the state, or you can ask your state real estate commission for a list.

#### *Seniors Real Estate Specialist (SRES)*

The SRES designation helps you understand the special housing and financial needs of senior citizens who are buying or selling residential real estate or investment properties. It helps agents understand tax issues that are important to seniors.

#### *Council of Real Estate Brokerage Managers (CRB)*

The CRB designation is awarded to Realtors® upon completion of a combination of extensive real estate managerial experience and formal training. Possessing certain other special designations allows you to bypass a portion of the study required for the CRB.

### *Council of Residential Specialists (CRS)*

The CRS designation is the highest professional designation a Realtor® can achieve in the field of residential sales. It is awarded after successful completion of six, two-day classes and a passing grade on the accompanying tests. Partial class credit is given for a bachelor's degree, for possession of some other special designations, and for verifiable experience as a successful real estate agent.

### *Accredited Buyer Representative (ABR)*

Receiving the ABR designation indicates that you have completed course work and experience to help you understand the special needs of real estate buyers. The designation is managed by the Real Estate Buyer's Agent Council (REBAC). Two days of course work is required but the designation is not awarded until you show proof that you have represented a certain number of buyer clients in completed transactions. Ongoing education is required for continued membership.

### *Graduate Realtor Institute® (GRI)*

GRI is a designation awarded after successful completion of three, four-day courses that cover many aspects of real estate, including sales and marketing, legal and regulatory issues, communications and technology, and professional standards requirements. GRI course work varies from state to state. Contact your State Association of Realtors® for information about classes in your area.

### *Additional Designations*

There are other useful designations you can earn through classroom and home study. Specialized classes are available for agents who wish to be property managers, for agents who plan to specialize in land sales, and for those who want to learn more about selling commercial or international properties. The NAR Web site, at *www.realtor.org*, is a good place to begin researching special designations.

### *Why a Designation?*

Although the general public may not understand the energy and commitment that go into receiving a designation, the benefits to your understanding of the real estate business are invaluable. It also becomes a source of referrals. Agents who know how hard a designation is to obtain will perceive you as more committed and may send you referrals.

### Nonaccredited Continuing Education

There are hundreds, if not thousands, of classes available beyond the classes needed to keep your license active. Seeking education beyond what is required can give you a competitive edge. From community colleges to traveling seminar speakers, as a real estate agent, you will be offered many opportunities to learn. Some will be very beneficial to your career but not all of them will meet your state's requirements for continuing education. This does not mean you should ignore nonaccredited continuing-education classes.

**E Alert**

> Most traveling seminar speakers do not make their money on the actual class, but on the materials they sell you after the class is over such as books, tapes, and systems. It is easy to get caught up in the promotion of these items and see them as the silver bullet to success. Be careful of what you purchase.

Be selective and take classes you believe will help, even if they do not earn you continuing-education credit. You may want to take a computer class or a time management class. You might attend a motivational class that is designed for any sales career, real estate or otherwise. Ask other agents if they have taken the classes being advertised, and what they thought of them.

### Cross-Training in Related Fields

As they spend time working in real estate, agents sometimes become interested in related professions, such as real estate appraisal and mortgage brokerage. Others become interested in related technical careers, such as home inspection and boundary surveying. Some who explore other interests enter the new career full-time but retain their agent's license, even if they don't plan to use it immediately, so they don't have to go through a lengthy licensing process again.

Acquiring education in related fields gives you a much deeper knowledge of the world of real estate, but it's sometimes difficult to work two careers at the same time. Keeping up with the laws and changes in each area can be time consuming and there are also other issues to consider, including conflicts of interest between your chosen fields.

### *Appraisers*

An appraiser's job is to determine a property's market value, usually furnishing the information to a lender or a cash buyer so that the funds provider knows the property is worth at least the amount of its purchase price. Contracts often move forward or die based on appraisal results, so the reports must be produced by someone who is honest and has nothing to gain or lose if the numbers aren't as expected.

Think about this. If you are the listing or selling agent or if you work for the listing or selling firm, could you provide an unbiased appraisal (one that doesn't favor any party) in the transaction? The answer is probably yes, but you *shouldn't take the assignment.* An appraiser who also works as an agent must sometimes turn down jobs in order to avoid the appearance of impropriety.

Appraisers are licensed by their state. They take specialized classroom instruction, just as a potential agent does, and must pass a state test. However, most appraisers do not become fully licensed until they have completed a lengthy internship, working under the supervision of a licensed appraiser. A typical internship requires each trainee to complete a certain number of appraisals or hours on the job.

#### Fact

Many large real estate firms provide a variety of in-house services for their clients, including appraisal and loan solutions, home inspections, and other services required to get a transaction to closing. Disclosing this "affiliated business arrangement" is critical, even if the buyer or seller does not use the in-house service.

Becoming a licensed appraiser gives you extra insight into the true market value of properties, knowledge that is an important tool when you work with buyers and sellers. Investigate your state's licensing requirements to help you determine if pursuing an appraisal license makes sense for you.

### *Mortgage Brokers*

Mortgage brokers bring buyers and lenders together. They are not loan officers, who work with the loan products at a single bank. They are independent agents who often have hundreds of lender contacts, making it possible for them to find a lender suitable for any type of credit situation. Mortgage brokers are paid a fee by the lender when a buyer obtains a loan.

Real estate agents who are also mortgage brokers are privy to a buyer's financial information and that knowledge could be a conflict if the buyers become interested in one of your listings. Would you tell the seller that the buyer is qualified for a loan that is larger than the price they offered for the property? You shouldn't, but will buyers wonder if you kept their personal information confidential?

One possible solution is to stop taking listings so that you don't deal directly with sellers. Build your business strictly on buyer services, advertising that you can help with both needs. Another solution is to refer any buyer interested in your listings to another mortgage broker.

#### Essential

Agents and firms who offer multiple services should not imply to customers and clients that they must use those services—that is called *steering*, and it is illegal. Always give buyers and sellers a list of at least three potential providers for each service.

Your state banking commission regulates mortgage brokers. That is the best place to find information about licensing requirements and ongoing support.

### *Other Related Careers*

Home inspections and land surveying are fields you might find interesting. Both require a great deal of technical training and expertise. Surveyors are licensed by their states. Home inspectors must be licensed in some states. You may also wish to specialize by working for a developer in new home sales only. Agents who work for a developer usually sell only the product that the developer is offering. They often receive a regular paycheck as well as a small commission on each unit sold. These agents do not always join the National Association of Realtors® since they do not use the MLS or other services it provides.

## Real Estate Conferences and Expositions

You'll have the opportunity to attend a variety of conferences and expositions (expos)—events held especially for real estate agents and people working in related occupations. Many of these events include educational opportunities and large numbers of vendors who set up booths to show you their products, which include everything from business cards to software to personal improvement programs.

### Question

**What's so important about getting to know agents in other cities?**

Other agents are useful as referral contacts. If you have a client who wants to move to a nearby city, wouldn't it be nice to know a good agent at their destination whom you feel comfortable referring them to? And one who will give you a referral fee for sending them the business?

The NAR holds an annual conference for Realtors®, and each state puts on a Realtor® expo at the state level. These are major events that draw some of the top names in teaching, plus the manufacturers of some of the best products to help you run your business.

Your local Board of Realtors® will likely hold smaller conferences, independently or in conjunction with other boards in the region.

Attending those seminars is an important way to keep in touch with real estate on a more local level.

Real estate prelicensing schools sometimes offer teaching seminars that focus on learning the business of real estate, rather than their usual licensing focus. Well-known teachers travel to larger cities to hold conferences of their own. Some franchises, such as Century 21, Coldwell Banker, and Prudential, hold annual conferences for their agents.

Attending seminars is the best way to find out which franchises offer the most valuable resources, and you'll learn something at every function you attend. You'll also get a valuable bonus—the ability to network with other agents. Having a pool of agents you can rely on for support and expertise is one of the best ways to move forward in your real estate career.

### Learning On the Job

On-the-job training is where real estate agents really learn their trade. Most of your real estate training will take place as you work with clients. No two transactions are the same. Each one has the potential to teach you how to deal with an entirely different set of conditions. You'll learn to be a mediator and a counselor. You'll learn to juggle schedules so that inspections and other necessary work are accomplished in a timely way and in the correct order.

If your real estate firm offers training classes, take advantage of them. If it doesn't, watch the experienced, successful agents, and try to determine why they are so successful. Are they good salespeople or do they know how to manage their time wisely? Are they agents who have a system to help them track customers? You'll find that successful agents have developed a system that helps them keep in touch with every person who contacts them.

If you have the chance to be a part of a mentor program, where more-experienced licensees train the less experienced, this is a great way to get a jump-start on real-life situations. In a mentor program, you will often share your commission with a more-experienced agent but you will also have the benefit of that agent's expertise to shorten your learning curve. Even if your office does not offer a mentor program, you may want to ask one of the top-producing agents if you can train with her in exchange for sharing some of your earnings.

**Essential**

> New agents often start their careers as a paid, licensed assistant to a top-producing agent. This gives them the chance to learn while in a salaried position. Some choose to stay in the assistant position and others eventually become independent, taking with them some tools for success.

The real estate business is constantly changing and the competition has always been strong. Coupled with experience, education can help to level the playing field. Constantly strive to better yourself, learn everything you can to set yourself ahead of the competition, and focus on success.

Chapter 3

# Getting Started in Real Estate

**A large percentage** of new real estate agents quit before they reach their first anniversary. There are many reasons why the dropout rate is high, but choosing the wrong firm to work for ranks near the top of the list. Choosing a firm that offers a good blend of training, moral support, and expense sharing can help ensure that you'll be around next year and that your business will continue to grow.

## *What Do You Want to Accomplish?*

Having unrealistic expectations about how much money you will make and how quickly you will succeed is another reason that many agents drop out after less than a year. Your own expectations are a part of what keeps you in the business or causes you to change careers, but your family's expectations are a part of this equation as well. If your family is uncomfortable with your hours and irregular paychecks, they can pressure you into quitting.

Developing a successful real estate career is closely linked to both your desire to succeed and your ability to stick with the job long enough for the elements required for success to fall into place. The process isn't easy or quick but you can give it a dramatic jump-start by setting goals for yourself, monitoring your accomplishments, and raising your own expectations a bit every time a goal is met.

As soon as you receive your real estate license in the mail, if not before, make goal setting a regular routine. Start by outlining some of the things you want to accomplish within the first thirty days, such as:

- Be established with an excellent firm.
- Notify all friends and family members that you can help them with their real estate needs.

- Join at least one local organization that helps you network with other professionals.
- Introduce yourself to mortgage brokers and loan officers at area banks.
- Begin working with at least two clients.

A career goal that is important to one agent may be on the bottom of the list for others, but one goal is universal: the desire to earn a good wage. Goal setting is the way to get there. You can't succeed without a plan. Begin by building a network of friends and professional contacts, then top that off with training. Vow to provide excellent service to all the clients you encounter, so that they will recommend you to others.

A written plan gives you a tangible reference. It makes the goals real, not simply random tasks you intend to take care of someday. As you become more familiar with your new career, keep working at it and adjusting your goals (see Chapter 4: Goal Setting and Lead Generation for more information on choosing and attaining your career goals).

## *Pre-Interview Research*

Choosing an agency affiliation is one of the most important decisions that every new licensee must make. Agents sometimes get into a pattern of switching agencies on a regular basis, trying to find the elusive "perfect" place to work. There is nothing wrong with moving on when an agency isn't what you expected it to be, but because stability helps past clients find you, staying put translates to dollars in your pocket. You'll be ahead of the game if you choose carefully the first time and find a firm that suits your short- and long-term needs.

You have probably made a mental list of agencies to consider. As you progressed through licensing school, that list might have shrunk or grown as you networked with other students and licensed agents. If everyone makes the same negative comments about a specific agency, you can assume that at least some of the concerns are valid. However, don't discount an agency if only one person has a problem with the company.

## E-Alert

Real estate is a very competitive field. Sometimes personalities clash and force agents to move on to another firm, leaving them with negative feelings about the incident. Keep the stories you hear in the back of your mind but form your own opinions during interviews.

Hopefully you have been paying attention to local real estate ads and for sale signs. Are there a few agencies that appear to have the majority of area listings? Firms that dominate your area market aren't necessarily the best places for a new agent to work, but their presence in the real estate market makes them agencies to at least consider.

You'll feel more comfortable asking and answering questions if you arrive for interviews with a basic understanding of each agency's public image, including its advertising practices and reputation in the community. Start narrowing down your list, asking yourself the following questions:

- Which firms produce professional-looking, interesting ads?
- Which firms have a good Internet presence?
- Which firms provide handouts at local visitor's centers or Chambers of Commerce?
- Do firms provide agent contact information within ads, making it easy for people to find you?
- Do any firms advertise on television or on the radio?
- Which firms offer training?
- What is the atmosphere of the office?
- Do they have a high agent turnover rate, or do people have a tendency to stay there?
- How are the phones handled? Do you get a machine or a real person when you call? Are they friendly and helpful?
- What is the broker like? The manager? Are they approachable?
- What type of market share does the office have?
- How do they handle referrals? Do they go to the top producer of the office or does everyone have an opportunity?

Pay close attention to every aspect of an agency's image, as well as its working environment to help determine which one might fit best with your own ideals.

### Assess Your Needs

If you live in a small town, where every agency sells real estate throughout the area, a real estate firm's location might not matter to you. Agents in larger cities might prefer to work with a company that specializes in neighborhoods that are either close to their homes or in other areas they are very familiar with.

Ask yourself these questions:

- Must I work close to home in order to be near my children, pets, or other family members who need care?
- Is there a specific area of town that I know well and would feel most confident working in?
- Do I have more potential client contacts in one area than in others?

Evaluate your personal needs in order to narrow down the number of firms you would like to consider.

## *Getting Ready for an Interview*

Interviewing for a real estate agent position is probably different from job interviews you have had in the past. When numerous applicants are vying for one opening, it's important to convince the interviewer that you are the best choice for the job. Real estate agencies interview many candidates. They're not trying to fill one position with the best applicant; they are trying to fill the entire office with the best (most productive, most promising) agents. You do want to make a good impression during your interview, but it is every bit as important for the agency to impress you.

Find out as much as you can about the agency before your interview. Its ads might tell you if the agency specializes in certain types of properties and ads should also reveal how many agents are already on staff. If possible, talk to a current agent to gather basic information—but don't make too many judgments about the agency until you've had a chance to speak with the broker-in-charge or the recruiter. Try to determine the normal dress code before your interview so that you dress appropriately. Plan to wear professional business attire if you cannot find out what is acceptable ahead of time.

### Fact

Real estate agencies are nearly always in a recruiting mode. Many will accept as many licensed agents as space allows in exchange for floor duty (helping out with phone chores and walk-in customers). The agency incurs little short-term cost if you do not succeed, so they are willing to offer you desk space while they evaluate your performance.

## *What Can They Offer You?*

You've made it through licensing school and passed your state exam, but do you really know what it's like to be a real estate agent? Don't feel bad if the answer is "no." It's a career you won't truly understand until you begin working at a firm, where you'll be exposed to many situations. To do that, it's essential to choose the right agency—not necessarily the largest or busiest agency in town but an office where many positive elements come together to create a good working environment for new agents and, most important, for you.

Take a legal pad or other type of tablet with you to the interview. You have many questions to ask and the only way to remember important details is to jot down the answers immediately.

### Does the Firm Provide Training?

All new agents need real-world training. Your licensing class covered the legal aspects of being an agent but it didn't teach you how to deal with real estate buyers and sellers. That is something you'll learn on the job, and you'll discover that real estate firms offer varying levels of training. Some firms have one or more agents who act as mentors or conduct in-house training sessions on a regular or as-needed basis. Larger agencies often hire trainers to help their new and seasoned agents. Franchised agencies that are part of a large network sometimes have regional schools, where you can attend intensive training sessions. Some firms pay all or a portion of your tuition costs for approved schools.

### E Alert

Find out how many agents the firm brought onboard during the previous year and how many of those are still around. While some loss is to be expected, if more than 50 percent of last year's new agents have moved on, it might be a signal that the firm does not offer good opportunities for beginners.

If the firm offers no training at all, it might be best to put it on the bottom of your list unless you determine that its other benefits outweigh the downside of seeking and paying for outside training.

### Errors and Omissions Insurance

Errors and omissions coverage, called E&O, is a type of liability insurance for real estate agents. It helps pay for the legal costs that you incur when someone believes you did not represent them as you should have and follows through with a lawsuit. It also pays a portion of resulting judgments or settlements. Even if you did absolutely nothing wrong, you can accumulate a great deal of debt while defending yourself, so the insurance is a must.

Find out if the firm provides E&O coverage for its agents. If so, how much coverage and what is the cost? (You can read more about E&O insurance in Chapter 14.)

### Leads for Agents

Does the agency give buyer and seller leads to new agents? Leads are the names and contact information for people who are interested in buying or selling real estate. The leads passed on to agents are usually people who have called or stopped by the office to ask a question without asking for a specific agent. Leads often come to you during floor duty, hours that you work in the office to help people who call or walk in. Ask several questions to learn how the firm's agents receive leads:

- Are all agents scheduled for floor duty?
- How often will you have floor duty?
- Are phone leads and walk-ins given to agents who are on duty when the leads occur?
- How does the agency distribute leads when messages are left on the office's answering machine or in its general voice mail?
- How are referrals from offices in other locations handled?

Buyer and seller leads are crucial to your success. If you find they are distributed on a seniority basis or if they go to the firm's owner, put the agency at the bottom of your list.

**Essential**

You might be surprised how many leads come your way on *all* days you are in the office, not just during your scheduled duty hours. Duty agents must sometimes leave for last-minute appointments or they get tied up in other ways. If you're there and ready to step in, those new buyer and seller leads could be yours.

### Computers and Other Tech Equipment

Computer equipment is a must for today's real estate agent. You'll likely access area listings on an Internet-based system, and lead-tracking software makes it much easier to keep track of your clients.

Having your own desktop or portable laptop makes the job easier, but does the agency provide computers and printers for agents to use at the office? What types of software are available on the main office computers?

How about a digital camera for taking photos of listings or previewing properties for buyers? Is there a scanner you can use to prepare print photos for e-mails and the Internet? If the firm does not provide them for agent use, plan to purchase a computer, digital camera, and other important equipment as soon as possible.

## *Your Ongoing Expenses*

Working as a nonemployee gives real estate agents a great deal of freedom to make their own schedules, but that independence also means they are responsible for nearly every expense related to doing business. The list of items they must pay for varies a great deal from agency to agency. You cannot compare firms until you know which ongoing expenses they pay.

### Fact

Some real estate firms charge a monthly desk fee—rental for the office space you occupy. You might even have to provide your own desk and other office furniture. Rental arrangements are more appropriate for a seasoned agent who has regular income. New agents have a harder time making those payments, because it takes a while before commissions kick in.

Ongoing expenses can take a bite out of your income every month, but the size of that bite varies greatly from agency to agency. Some companies expect agents to purchase all of their office supplies, including stamps and photocopies. What about computer paper and ink cartridges, file folders, note pads—are those items you must buy? Long-distance calls made from the office can be a significant monthly expense if you must pay for them.

Try to think of all the expenses you might incur on a regular basis and ask which costs the agency pays.

### Advertising Expense

Every successful real estate firm advertises itself and its listings. You've seen ads in local real estate booklets, where photos of homes and other properties are accompanied by descriptive text. Does the agency pay for those ads or must agents pay a share to have their listings included?

What about classified ads in local newspapers? Are they an agent expense or does the firm offer help? Overall, what types of advertising does the firm cover?

**Essential**

Many real estate firms have a bulk-mailing permit that allows them to send large quantities of advertising material at a reduced postage rate. Agents are typically allowed to use the permit if they pay for the postage. Ask your interviewer about company policy for use of its permit.

### Multiple Listing Service Fees

If the firm is a member of a local Board of Realtors® and Multiple Listing Service (MLS), their membership agreement usually requires that all affiliated agents become members as well. The agent nearly always pays for MLS and board fees. Developers, who only sell their own properties, may not be members of the MLS. There are also offices, usually in rural areas, who choose not to be members of the National Association of Realtors® and sell only their own listings. Some regions of the country have an MLS system that is not affiliated with the National Association of Realtors® so that, although other agents can access it, it is not available on the Internet via *www.realtor.com*.

Firms that offer services in multiple areas often belong to more than one MLS service and you'll have to decide if membership in multiple areas is required to work effectively with clients.

Some fees are paid on a yearly basis, but others might be billed monthly or quarterly. Ask your interviewer about the expenses associated with required and optional memberships.

## *How Are You Paid?*

Nearly all real estate agents are paid commissions, which is a percentage of the funds earned by the firm at the end of a real estate transaction. The commission percentage offered to agents is one area where you will see a great deal of variation between agencies. It's critical to get the numbers straight before you accept a position.

Some real estate newcomers think the entire commission paid by a client goes to the person who sells the property. That can happen, but it's rare. The fee paid by a listing client is typically split four times, with portions going to:

- The listing firm
- The listing agent
- The selling firm
- The selling agent

If one firm or agent lists and sells, they are said to have *both sides* of the transaction, meaning they will be paid for two portions of the split.

Your interviewer can give you three important figures: the average sales price of a property in your area, the typical commission percentage paid by a client, and the percentage of the firm's portion that you are paid. From those figures, you can make some estimates by referring to Chapter 15: Managing Your Finances.

### Question

**What should I ask the firm when I am interviewed?**
Ask how many agents work in your area and how many homes were sold there last year. The answers will give you a feel for activity in the local real estate market and help you see how many people are sharing in the sales figures. The figure might not include lots, land, and commercial properties.

Questions you should ask about commissions include:

- **Are commissions paid on a sliding scale?** Some agencies increase your percentage rate as your sales climb. The rate usually reverts back to the original percentage at the beginning of each year or on the anniversary of your hire date.
- **When are commissions paid?** Most firms pay agents on the day a transaction is completed, but some firms take several days for processing.
- **Will you earn a higher commission for in-house transactions?** Some agencies pay a slightly higher percentage when the property sold is one of their own listings.
- **Is there a franchise commission?** Agents working for franchised agencies, such as Century 21, Prudential, and Coldwell Banker, usually pay a fee back to the franchising company at each closing to pay for national advertising.
- **Is there an advertising fee for local advertising?** Some companies charge each agent for in-office advertising.
- **Is there desk rent?** Some offices charge a minimum monthly fee, known as desk rent. This fee is often waived if the agent is producing commissions.
- **Are there any other fees that may be deducted from your commission?** Some offices have a transaction coordinator who makes sure all paperwork is filled out correctly, the terms of the contract are adhered to, and all timelines are met. Transaction coordinators are paid a set fee for each transaction that closes.
- **Is there a policies and procedures manual?** Not all offices have a policies and procedures manual, but if the office you are considering does have one, be sure you have the opportunity to read it before you make a final decision.

Commission comparisons are an important consideration when you're searching for the best agency, but they are not the most critical issue to consider. Agencies that pay a high commission rate but offer few services and leads for agents are not nearly as attractive as firms that offer a lower rate but plenty of leads and other help. Would you rather have 60 percent of very few sales or 50 percent of many?

## Franchise vs. Independent Agency

Independent real estate agencies are companies that operate on their own, without a network of affiliated firms, making decisions about every aspect of the business. Franchise agencies have quite a bit of freedom in their operations but must stick to the basic guidelines of the company with which they are associated.

There are pros and cons for affiliation with a franchise. Some agents refuse to be affiliated with a franchised firm because of the commission that is paid back to the company with every closed transaction. The fee can take 8 percent or more from each paycheck. Over time, it amounts to a hefty sum. A number of franchises also charge agents additional fees on a monthly or quarterly basis.

### Fact

You likely recognize the names of the major real estate franchises, such as Century 21, ERA, Coldwell Banker, Prudential, Keller Williams, RE/MAX, and many others.

On the other hand, franchises usually offer agents access to professional-looking, discounted supplies, such as business cards, signs, and other important advertising materials. Some offer low-cost subscriptions to home-related magazines that can be used for client gifts. Many franchises have ties with mortgage lenders who make it easy for you to help your clients find a home loan. Franchises also have a built-in referral network for clients moving to or from your area.

Each agent must weigh the advantages and disadvantages of working for a franchise. In most cases, it makes no difference at all if a firm is an independent or a franchise agency. The success of the individual agency and the perks it can offer you are the most important things to consider when seeking a real estate position.

The pros and cons of working for an independent office are more subtle. How is their advertising handled? What type of image have they developed for themselves? Do they receive referrals from out-of-town offices? How much do marketing materials cost?

## The Final Decision

Once you have chosen a firm, make it an extension of your name: Anne Smith with Prudential or Jim Taylor with ABC Realty. As a new agent, connecting your name to a firm with a good reputation automatically gives you a good reputation, too. You can use the leverage of your firm's good name to help you with clients and customers. You may be new, but you have the power of an established company behind you.

If you have chosen a firm and discover early on that it may not be the right choice for you, think about why you want to make a move. If you are having a personality conflict with one of the other agents, you may want give it some time to cool down. Remember, every office is full of personalities.

### E Alert

When you make the choice to change offices, remember that any listings you have belong to your broker and will likely need to stay with the office you are leaving. You will have to rebuild any leads you have generated and retrain your friends and family to find you and send you referrals.

If promises were made to you but those promises are not kept, it may be the right decision to change offices. Carefully consider your motivations for moving and be completely sure that you are doing the right thing for your career. Loyalty and consistency are looked on favorably, so be sure you are totally ready to make the move.

Success involves more than money. A friendly work environment, excellent training, expense-sharing, and fair commissions all come together to create the best choice for your needs.

Chapter 4

# Goal Setting and Lead Generation

**If you are** going to succeed in real estate, you must have a plan. Regardless of your motivation for entering the profession, success or failure in real estate lies squarely on your shoulders. It is important to know where you are going. It's always best to be prepared and it's never too early to determine your destination. Establishing clear goals will provide direction and smooth the road to achievement.

## *What Are Your Goals?*

If you have never been to a place, would you know how to get there without directions? You need know what you will do to get ahead in the business and you won't know where you are going without clear, written goals.

Goal setting is critical. Written goals are like a road map. In addition to providing direction, written goals give you a way to track your progress—so this is not an assignment to be completed and forgotten. You should consider it a long-term task and keep it on your to-do list indefinitely.

Clearly defined goals can help you make decisions at critical points every day. When presented with a problem, we often consider various options as solutions. When making these decisions, you can refer to your goals. Ask yourself what actions will bring you closer to your goals and what actions might move you further away.

For instance, if you are spending your floor time catching up on gossip with the other agents in the office but your goal is to sell three houses this month, focusing on the goal may get you back to your desk for prospecting calls rather than hanging out at the coffee pot, talking.

## Fact

Market conditions can affect your business, but you are the main reason you succeed or fail. There are plenty of agents making a great living in a very bad market by working toward their goals. Practice goal setting in a good market and when a bad market hits, you will not be as affected as other agents.

## Goals Must Be Written Down

Find yourself a yellow pad or a fancy journal; it doesn't matter where you write your goals down—it only matters that you do. Go someplace where you will not have any interruptions. Write down everything that you want to accomplish, either immediately or in the future.

Writing goals about real estate is only a part of the goal-writing process, you need to write your other goals as well. Of course, you are in the real estate business to be in the real estate business, but you are also in the business for the quality of life it affords. Making money is not enough. What is a ton of money worth if you have no family life, poor health, and no free time? You should set goals in all the areas of your life. Write goals for your health, your family and friends, your finances, your spiritual or religious practices, and any other areas of life that are important to you.

What does money mean to you? Does it mean being able to afford your kids' soccer uniforms and having time to go to the games? Does it mean getting a great car or owning some rental properties? Everyone has his own concept of a good, successful life. Make your choices and write them down, so you know where you're going.

Although some of your goals will be related to real estate, such as, "I want to sell twenty homes," you will also have other goals such as, "I want to go to Europe," or "I want to lose weight."

Once you have finished brainstorming, read your goals and rewrite them as affirmative statements in the present tense. Then, give each goal a specific deadline. For example, "I will sell twenty homes this year," "I am going to Europe in October," "I will lose fifteen pounds by my sister's wedding." Goals written in this clearly defined, affirmative way have the greatest impact. If you were to write them as desires, such as, "I *want* to sell twenty homes this year," "I *want* to go to Europe sometime," "I *will try* to lose fifteen pounds," they turn into wishes, rather than actual goals. Vague goals are nothing more than dreams, and they do not help you move forward. As you rewrite your goals, determine what they will cost you to accomplish. This cost needs to be measured in time as well as in financial terms.

**Essential**

With respect to real estate, your plan can include goals for income, education, ranking in your office and the community, a certain number of contacts on your mailing list, a certain number of transactions for the year, or a goal to grow your business and hire an assistant.

## *Breaking Down Your Goals*

Sort your goals into categories, identifying them as short term, mid-range, or long range. Some goals can be accomplished within a few weeks or months; other goals will take years to accomplish. Focus on what you can do today to further each of the goals you have set. The easiest way to do that is to break down your goals into doable segments. Let's start with the goal of selling twenty homes this year:

1. How many people do you have to contact to find one buyer or one seller?

2. How many potential buyers do you have to work with to find one that actually buys within thirty days?

3. How many listing presentations do you have to go on before you get a listing?

4. How long does it take for that listing to sell?

Telephone prospecting is just one of the ways that you can generate business. Telephone prospecting, especially with people you know, has proven to be a quick and effective way to generate business and it should be included in your goal-setting activities. "Cold calls" are telephone calls to people with whom you have no previous relationship. Your telephone strategy to achieve your goals of acquiring buyers, sellers, and listings should be comprised of either many cold calls or fewer warm calls (calls to people with whom you have a previous relationship).

A sample telephone prospecting plan may look like this:

**Cold Calls**

- Make five calls a day for twenty days to receive 100 contacts.
- Assume that from every 100 contacts you make, you receive one buyer.
- Assume that one out of five buyers will buy within thirty days.

With this formula you will need to make 10,000 cold calls to sell twenty homes.

**Warm Calls**

- Make five calls a day for twenty days to receive 100 contacts.
- Assume that for every 100 contacts you make, you receive ten buyers.
- Assume that one out of five buyers will buy within thirty days.

With this formula you will need to make 2,000 warm calls to sell twenty homes.

## Question

**What if one of my goals is to win the lottery?**

By breaking down your goal into manageable chunks you may discover that winning the lottery is a 1 in 10 million chance. If this is the case, how many lottery tickets do you need to purchase to guarantee you the win?

A sample telephone prospecting plan for securing a listing may look like this:

### Cold Calls

- Make five calls a day for twenty days to receive 100 contacts.
- Assume that out of every 100 contacts you make, you receive one listing presentation.
- Assume that one out of five listing presentations culminates in a listing.

With this formula you will need to make 10,000 cold calls to list twenty homes. From here you need to figure out market time in your area to see how long it will take these listings to sell.

### Warm Calls

- Make five calls a day for twenty days to receive 100 contacts.
- Assume that for every 100 contacts you make, you receive ten listing presentations.
- Assume that one out of five listing presentations culminates in a listing.

With this formula you will need to make 2,000 warm calls to list twenty homes. From here you need to figure out market time to see how long it will take these listings to sell.

In a good market, you may be able to make fewer calls, half as many or less, to accomplish your goals. In a tough market, it may take more calls to accomplish your goals. The "warmer" your warm calls are, the fewer calls you will need to make to secure a buyer or a listing.

When breaking down your goals into daily actions, set aside time, every day, for telephone prospecting. In the previous example you may have "make five prospecting calls every day" as one of your goals.

### Farming

This type of prospecting is designed to "cultivate" leads over a period of time. Generally speaking, farming does not generate leads quickly but if performed consistently, it will produce results over the long term.

Start by choosing a farm area. Your farm area can be a geographical farm, such as a particular subdivision, condominium complex, or neighborhood. Your farm area can also be a nongeographical farm, such as people you know, tenants, or business owners.

Once you have decided on a farm you will need to "work the farm." Sending regular mailers with information that your farm will find helpful is a part of the process. Geographical farms may include statistics on the neighborhood or news of an upcoming homeowner's association meeting. If you are farming a condominium complex, attend the homeowner's meetings and add their information to your mailers. If you are farming tenants, you may want to send them information about the latest loan program that can help them get qualified to purchase a home. When farming business owners, you may want to concentrate on good investments in the real estate marketplace.

No matter what type of farm you have, it is important to give all the prospects within the farm something worth keeping, along with your photo and contact information. If they keep and use the item you send, your prospects will view your picture and contact information repeatedly over a period of time. This will make your name recognizable and synonymous with real estate in their minds.

**Essential**

Examples of items you can give to the community you are farming are a monthly recipe card, a magnet with the local sport team's schedule, or a wallet-sized tipping chart. All of these items give you the opportunity to keep your name fresh in the minds of the individuals you seek as clients.

Farming will rarely produce results overnight. Most people receive piles of mail and may not notice your mailer unless they are specifically looking for a real estate agent. You can increase the value of your farming with follow-up calls and (in a geographical farm) by being visible in the neighborhood.

### Door Knocking

When used in conjunction with a neighborhood farm, door knocking can increase your results. Going house to house and greeting people at their door, checking to be sure they received your mailer and asking them if they are in need of any real estate services, will make you the one person they think of if they are selling in your area.

Expanding on this by holding neighborhood block parties, delivering flags on the Fourth of July, or pumpkins at Halloween can establish your image as the agent who knows the neighborhood.

If you are farming a neighborhood, making a breakdown goal to expand your marketing activities beyond mailings will give you a consistent presence. These goals might include, "knock on ten doors every Saturday," "deliver seasonal gifts to the farm every two months," or "hold a block party once each summer."

### Open Houses

Holding an open house can be a good way to generate leads. If you do not have a listing of your own, you can volunteer to hold an open house for one of the other agents in your office. Many sellers believe that an open house will sell their house. However, it is actually more of a lead generator for the agent holding the open house than for the seller. It is more likely that you will find a buyer for another property than for the property you are showing. You may also receive a lead for a listing, as other potential sellers often check out their competition before placing their house on the market.

### Fact

To make the open house experience pleasurable for visitors and beneficial for you, serve cookies and coffee or some other goodies. Have a guest book for people to sign so that you can have a resource of potential client names.

To make the most of an open house, you will want to get prepared in advance. Send an invitation to the neighborhood to visit your open house on the day and time you have scheduled. This can either be mailed or delivered via door hangers. Bring flyers for the open house, as well as for other available properties in the area. Be knowledgeable about the market. People at open houses will often ask a lot of questions in order to size you up and decide if you are the agent they want to use. Bring maps and outline other potential houses in the area. Be sure to have visible open house signs directing people to the property.

When breaking down your goals you may want to include "hold an open house every Sunday afternoon."

## Floor Time

Like an open house, you are waiting for business. If you have the opportunity to take floor time (sometimes known as *up time* or *opportunity time*), this may be a time that you can receive a lead or two. You will likely be in charge of the phones, taking messages for other agents, or setting up appointments for showings. Hopefully, you will get a call about some of the office advertising or someone who is interested in real estate will walk in off the street to ask questions. In your goal breakdown you can write, "take floor time twice a week."

## Business Contacts

Getting to know business owners who may refer prospects to you is a long-term source of business. Perhaps you regularly frequent a certain coffeehouse or retail shop. Let them know you are in the real estate business and see if you can take the owner to lunch. Ask them for referrals as you send referrals to them. Be sure to cultivate those relationships, not only for the quality of the relationship but for the potential of referrals as well. In your breakdown of goals you may want to write, "take a business owner to lunch every week."

Look at your goals that aren't related to real estate and break them into manageable chunks, too. As an example, let's break down the goal of going to Europe in October.

- How much does it cost to go to Europe? Think about:

  Airline tickets
  Hotel
  Meals
  Spending money

- Add up the expenses of the trip. Assuming the trip costs $5,000 and assuming that October is ten months away, you will need to set aside $500 per month toward your European vacation.
- How long will I be gone?
- Who will handle my business while I am away?

Let's break down the goal of losing fifteen pounds by the wedding:

- The wedding is in three months.
- I need to lose five pounds per month.
- This is 1.25 pounds per week.
- In order to lose 1.25 pounds per week, I need to increase my exercise by twenty minutes per day and cut calories by 300 per day.
- This means walking every night after dinner and no dessert until after the wedding.

## A Business Plan

Once you have your goals written and organized, they will become the start of your business plan. Yes, you probably work in an office with other agents and a supervising broker, but you are responsible for your income. Essentially, you own your own business and all successful business owners have a business plan.

In general, the simplest approach is usually the best. It's easy to get bogged down with details and it's possible to devote too much time to this. That can happen if it is the first time you've addressed this type of project. There are myriad books available on the subject of goal setting and business plans.

### Fact

*The One Page Business Plan* by Jim Horan offers a simple format for creating your vision, mission, objectives, strategies, and a plan of action so that you can sculpt an organized and goal-centered foundation for your business.

Whatever form you choose, it's important to devote enough energy to this so that the resulting plan holds meaning for you and provides direction, without spending so much time on the plan that you lose focus on actually doing the business. (Learn more about how to create a business plan in Chapter 19.)

## Keeping On Track

The road to real estate success is complicated to navigate, even if you have a good map. The key to staying on track is keeping that map open and available, so you can refer to it whenever you need help with the next step. The question to ask yourself is always, "What will bring me closer to achieving my goals?"

As you progress in this business, you may find that your goals change. Perhaps your original plan didn't include enough time with your family. Maybe your original income or education goals were set too low. Perhaps a little experience has shown you an area of specialization you would like to investigate. Update your plan and keep it fluid. Make changes to accommodate your growth and the experience you will accumulate as a professional. You must always have a plan, but you don't need to rigidly stick to the plan you made as a beginner.

## Hiring a Coach

If you have trouble setting goals, creating a business plan, or implementing the plan you've created, you may want to consider hiring a coach. Coaches are not just for athletes; anyone who wants to be proficient in her field would do well to hire a coach. Over the last several years, personal coaching has become more and more mainstream. Rather than going to a seminar and hearing a great idea once, many seminar companies have branched into coaching. Others have started as coaching companies but add the benefit of seminars, so they can reach a broader audience. A coach will help you with the fundamentals, teach you how to work with your particular strengths, keep you on track, and make you accountable for the action steps required for success.

### E Alert

Sometimes it is possible to tell if an agent has a coach. Look for top-producing agents who have had a decent career at a lower level, but who have recently vaulted to a dramatically higher level of success.

There are coaches who specialize in real estate, coaches who specialize in all types of sales, and coaches who specialize in general business. There are also coaches, called "life coaches," who help you with a larger overview.

You can learn about which coaching program would be best for you by asking other agents for referrals. Ask the top producers in your office if they have a coach. Check with top-producing lenders as well. Go to the real estate conventions, listen to the national speakers, and see if their style appeals to you. Most of them have coaching programs or can refer you to one that they find beneficial. You can also meet with agents from other areas at these conventions and ask for their input.

You can also search the Internet for a coach. Typing "real estate coaching" or "life coaching" into your Web browser will produce pages and pages of potential coaches. If you'd rather not wade through voluminous numbers of coaching companies, asking for a referral from someone who has found success is an easier way. If you do not know anyone who can give you a referral, the following is an alphabetical list of some of the coaching programs available.

**Anthony Robbins:** *www.anthonyrobbins.com*
**Buffini and Company:** *www.brianbuffini.com*
**Howard Brinton:** *www.howardbrinton.com*
**Mike Ferry:** *www.mikeferry.com*
**Nightingale-Conant:** *www.nightingale.com*
**Steven Covey:** *www.franklincovey.com*
**Tom Hopkins International:** *www.tomhopkins.com*
**Walter Frey:** *www.waltfrey.com*
**Walter Sanford:** *www.waltersanford.com*

If you do not have the funds to hire a coach yet, you may want to consider a mentor program in your office. It is important to have someone, other than yourself, who can hold you accountable for performing the tasks you must complete to reach your goals.

## Essential

Coaching costs money. Those agents in a coaching program will tell you it is worth the expense, but a new agent may find the costs hard to swallow. If you decide to hire a coach, plan on budgeting between $400 and $500 per month. One good sale will usually pay the cost of the entire year of coaching.

## *Doing the Work*

Once you have set your goals and have broken those goals into manageable segments, you need to actually do the work it takes to achieve your goals. Your daily goals will not be to make a sale or to get a listing; your daily goals will be to prospect. Consistent prospecting produces consistent results, so take time every day to do prospecting. The habit will make your business more consistent.

Most agents prospect only when they are hungry. When they handle deals or have a client or customer, they forget prospecting and then start all over when they are hungry again. These ups and downs are harrowing and they do not produce a predictable income. The stress level is high and will make you feel like you're living on a roller coaster. Make it your habit to prospect every day. You will have a more predictable income and you will always have something in the pipeline. You can go from the roller coaster that most agents experience by only prospecting during the slow times, to just a few speed bumps as the market moves up and down.

Your daily list may look something like this:

1. Make five warm calls
2. Make ten cold calls
3. Send out ten mailers
4. Send out five notes to people who may refer business to you
5. Take a business owner or past client to lunch (and ask for referrals)

If you have set a goal and you do not reach it, this does not necessarily mean you have failed. It may mean you need more time to accomplish it. Like water wearing against a rock, consistent prospecting appears to be a slow process, but it will give you steady results. Complete the tasks necessary for success as you focus on your goals.

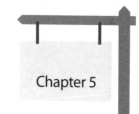

Chapter 5

# Time Management

**Having a flexible** schedule is a big motivator for going into real estate, but having that flexibility means that you must control your own time. If you don't, your clients and customers will control it for you and it will no longer be flexible. If you are tired of the Monday through Friday, nine-to-five grind and you want some flexibility, a real estate career can give you that—but only if you take control of your time.

## *Time-Blocking Your Priorities*

Start by blocking out your vacations. You don't want to cancel vacation because a big client is coming to town. You need to let that client know that you already have a commitment at that time. You are in control. If the client respects you, this will not be an issue. If the client does not respect you, why would you want to work with him? It may seem strange to block out vacations first, but having something to look forward to will make you more productive. It is often said that more work gets done the two weeks preceding a vacation than at any other time—and it is true. By planning when you are going to be gone, you will make better use of the remaining time.

Next, block out at least one day off per week. You can block out two half days if that is the best you can do. Without rest you will be weakened and not perform at an optimal level. If you are consistent about which day you take off, your clients will get used to it and you will not receive calls that day. Perhaps you start by taking off on Thursday afternoons and Sunday mornings. As your business grows, you may decide to take all day Thursday plus Sunday mornings. If you create a pattern that people can depend on, it will not be difficult to take the time off.

### Question

**I can't afford a vacation yet. Can I plan one later, after a few sales?**
If you are just starting in the business the cost of a vacation may not be in your budget—but plan one anyway. Visiting family or going camping, as long as you are not working, is still a vacation.

## *How to Make Your Schedule*

Block out everything you need to do for yourself as if it were a client appointment: 2:00 P.M. to 3:00 P.M., haircut; 3:15 to 5:00 P.M., soccer game; 6:00 P.M. to 7:00 P.M., dinner. Block out time for continuing education so that you can keep your license current. Block out time to cultivate new business: 8:00 A.M., Rotary breakfast; 9:30 to 11:00 A.M., prospecting calls. The time that is left is the time you will have for your clients. Your weekly schedule may look like this:

**Weekly Schedule**

| Monday | |
|---|---|
| 6:30 A.M. | Exercise |
| 8:00 A.M. | Rotary breakfast |
| 9:30–11:00 A.M. | Prospecting calls |
| 11:00–12:00 | Return calls and handle paperwork |
| 12:00–1:00 | Lunch |
| 1:00–4:00 | Client time |
| 4:00–5:00 | Return calls and handle paperwork |
| 5:00–6:30 | Client time |
| 6:30 | Dinner |

| | |
|---|---|
| **Tuesday** | |
| 6:30 A.M. | Exercise |
| 8:00–9:30 A.M. | Prospecting calls |
| 9:30–11:00 A.M. | Client time |
| 11:00–12:00 | Return calls and handle paperwork |
| 12:00–1:00 | Lunch |
| 1:00–3:00 | Client time |
| 3:00–5:00 | Kid's soccer game |
| 5:00–6:30 | Client time |
| 6:30 | Dinner |
| **Wednesday** | |
| 6:30 A.M. | Exercise |
| 8:00–9:30 A.M. | Return calls and handle paperwork |
| 9:30–12:00 | Client time |
| 12:00–1:00 | Lunch |
| 1:00–3:00 | Prospecting calls |
| 3:00–4:00 | Return calls and paperwork |
| 5:00–6:30 | Haircut |
| 6:30 | Dinner |
| **Thursday** | |
| 6:30 A.M. | Exercise |
| 8:00–6:30 | Time off |
| 6:30 | Dinner |
| **Friday** | |
| 6:30 A.M. | Exercise |
| 8:00–9:30 A.M. | Prospecting calls |
| 9:30–11:00 A.M. | Client time |
| 11:00–12:00 | Return calls and handle paperwork |
| 12:00–1:00 | Lunch |
| 1:00–4:00 | Continuing education class |
| 4:00–6:30 | Client time |
| 6:30 | Dinner |

| Saturday | |
|---|---|
| 8:00–9:30 A.M. | Breakfast with the family |
| 9:30–11:00 A.M. | Client time |
| 11:00–12:00 | Return calls and handle paperwork |
| 12:00–1:00 | Lunch |
| 1:00–4:00 | Client time |
| 4:00 | Leave office early |
| 6:30 | Dinner |
| **Sunday** | |
| 8:00–10:00 A.M. | Relax |
| 10:00–12:00 | Spiritual or religious practice |
| 12:00–1:00 | Lunch |
| 1:00–5:00 | Client time |
| 5:00–6:30 | Relax |
| 6:30 | Dinner |

If you allow your clients to manage your time for you, you will find yourself working a 24-7 schedule. You will have clients who want to see you on Sunday morning and you will be getting calls at 11:30 in the evening when your seller wakes up worried that his house hasn't sold. You will find your time gets filled up because you have an empty calendar. You must take control of your schedule before your clients do.

This is where time management becomes very important. You hear about real estate agents who work seven days a week. They arrive in the early morning to make their calls and organize their day. They work on paperwork and then the phones start ringing. They field calls and put out fires until late in the evening. They may show property when a client gets off work, and they skip dinner. These agents are always available. Their cell phone or pager is always going off as they jump from one thing to the next. This is not a controlled schedule and it is definitely not flexible. You need to make the rules.

## *Flexible Hours?*

Once new agents get into an office, they discover that their hours are not as flexible as they had hoped and the hours can also be quite long.

Agents are often ruled by the floor time schedule and the needs of their clients. You will surely find that your services are needed at odd hours and other areas of your life could suffer as your career takes off.

It's important to take control of your time from the beginning. This does not mean that you will not put in a ton of hours, working five, six, or even seven days a week, especially when you first start out. It does mean that *you* control your time; *no one else* should control your time. Of course, you will take floor time, be present in the office, hold open houses, show property, and perform all the tasks that add up to success, but you will also be in charge of your own time. Protect your time—before it gets filled up by things that do not contribute to your success or your quality of life.

If you create a schedule, you will also find that you are accomplishing the tasks on your to-do list instead of listening to the latest gossip or playing solitaire on the computer.

## *Time-Blocking in Your Personal Life*

Some choose this career to have more free time for their personal life and then get caught up in the hours and spend more and more time working. They do not take time off and their home life and health often suffer. One way to combat this is with time-blocking. This means that you will actually block out time in your schedule for the areas of your life that require attention. You must use your calendar to schedule your child's school play, your laundry, your nail appointment, your exercise routine, and your Friday night date with your spouse. These appointments are important and should be blocked out right along with your floor time and your open house schedule. Putting all business and personal appointments together will eliminate the possibility of double booking your time. It will also eliminate the need to apologize to your loved ones when you choose to show property instead of spending time with them. It may sound silly, but it's critical to start making your schedule work now. Schedule time for yourself and your personal life.

Your life is made up of many elements; your real estate career is only *one* of them. You need to maintain a balanced life in order to have the energy and presence of mind that your new business requires. As you develop your career, consider the other areas of life, including your health, family, and spiritual or religious practices.

### Your Health

You have heard the saying, "If you don't have your health, you don't have anything." As simple as it sounds, it is true. Regular exercise and good eating habits will go a long way toward keeping you in shape for the rigors of real estate, ensuring that your physical, mental, and emotional health is at its best.

Take time to exercise for at least a half-hour every workday. Block out the time in your calendar and stick with it. When you are doing your exercise, turn off your cell phone or pager and focus on the exercise. Let your mind rest and don't allow yourself to think about work for that small thirty-minute segment of your day.

**Essential**

You can even do some things to help your mental and emotional health during a busy workday. Take a small break every hour or two. Get up from your desk and stretch, walk outside, and look up at the sky or across the street. These breaks will revitalize you and make you more productive at the office.

Many people don't like breakfast or don't think they have time for it, but you need to make time to eat a good breakfast every day (coffee and a sweet roll don't count). It is optimal to eat several other small meals throughout the day, and to block out time for lunch as well. If you're worried that it won't be productive, bring a client along. Drink plenty of water. Constant dehydration can lead to long-term health issues. Keep some healthy snacks handy at your desk, such as fruit or granola bars, in case you are running from appointment to appointment. You can even pack a snack bag with some sandwiches or other snacks and bottled waters to share with your clients or customers when showing property. They'll probably get hungry too!

Just as important as your physical health is your mental and emotional health. Take time for yourself. Spend some of it doing nothing, just relaxing. Spend time on a hobby or interest that you have. Even if you block out a few hours once a week, you will find yourself revitalized by the practice. Read a book for fun, have a massage—anything that gives you pleasure will clear your mind and make you a better agent when you are working.

### Your Family and Friends

At the beginning of your real estate career, as you are gearing up to make a living, the people you will spend the least amount of time with are the ones you care about the most (because "they understand"). Your family and friends do understand—at first. After a while, they will feel neglected and unloved if you do not give them your time. Your time is the biggest gift you can give them, and having time for your friends and family is probably one of the reasons you chose this career. Block out time for them every day. Not just the "bye honey, I gotta run" time, but a phone call or a personal note, a cup of coffee, lunch, or time to go for a walk together. If you are perfectly successful in real estate but lose all the people who are important to you, why bother?

If your family lives in another community, make a habit of calling them from your cell phone on your way home, once or twice a week. It gears you down from the workday and gives you a chance to be in touch, if only for a few moments. Those few moments will mean a lot to your family and your relationship with them.

### Your Spiritual or Religious Practices

If you do not have a spiritual or religious practice, this can also mean your volunteer time or charity work. If you have never taken the time for any of these things, seek out and find something that interests you. You may spend time with Habitat for Humanity, building houses in your area. You may volunteer to read at a nursing home or you may enjoy volunteering at your child's school. When you give to something that is outside of yourself, you will often find the benefits to yourself far exceed what you have given.

You may believe that participation in these activities will also bring you clients and customers for your real estate business. While this is often the case, it should not be your motivating factor for participating. You should do these things for the personal value they bring to your life. Consider the potential of new business from these activities as a bonus, not as the reason for doing them.

## *Time-Blocking Regular Activities*

In order to build a business as a real estate agent, you will need to set aside time to perform the necessary tasks. It will seem as though there are never enough hours in the day but, as you become more proficient with the work that needs to be accomplished, you will have more and more time available. You will never be able to get everything done that you want to do, but you will accomplish everything that needs to get done.

E Alert

If you are a morning person, block out prospecting time in the morning. If you gear up in the afternoon, block out prospecting time then. These are the hours when you need to be most productive. Do prospecting when you are at your best. It will help you come across as more well-spoken, knowledgeable, and confident.

### Prospecting

The number one skill necessary to be successful in real estate is to have the ability to create business. This is what prospecting is all about. Prospecting includes making telephone calls, networking, and sending out mailers. It includes open houses and door knocking—in short, everything that has the potential to bring you business. Block out prospecting time every workday; it is the most important thing that you do.

## Using Floor Time Productively

Floor time, up time, or opportunity time—whatever name your office gives it, these are the hours you are asked to stay in the office and answer phones or otherwise be available for potential new business. This new business may come in due to your office's advertising, location, or reputation. It may be a phone call from someone who wants to buy or sell real estate or someone may walk into the office looking for an agent. Floor time can be productive but it can also be a few hours of nothing. Schedule your floor time but use those hours to continue prospecting. You may not be able to make phone calls, in case you are required to take calls from potential buyers and sellers, but you can address mailers, design flyers, or do other tasks that can be accomplished at any time. These tasks can be set aside if you do get new business from your floor time and they can be completed if you have nothing else to do.

## Open Houses

On a slow day, an open house may end up being as quiet as sitting in your own living room. On a busy day, you may have many people come through to see the property. If it is quiet, treat the open house like floor time and work on your mailers and flyers. If it is busy, get to know the people who come through. Offer to keep in touch and, if they agree, get their contact information. Put them in your database and follow up with them the next day, and on a regular basis after that.

## Showing Property

It is a little harder to block out specific time to show property than it is for floor time or open houses. You now have clients in the car and they have a schedule too. Some people look through homes quickly, eliminating the ones they don't like at a glance. Others may spend considerable time in each property. Let your buyer know up front how much time you have allotted to see property. You might say, "I have set aside three hours to look at homes today. We may not be able to see everything on our list but it has been my experience that, after three hours, it is harder to remember each individual house. If we need more time, we can get together and look again on Wednesday."

**Essential**

Showing property to prospective buyers is an appointment with a beginning and an end. Choose the properties carefully, prepare the route in advance, and let your clients know the schedule. They may linger at certain properties, but they will also be aware that their time is limited.

### Marketing

Set aside time for creating flyers and advertising, making calls to anyone who may be a buyer or have a buyer for your property. You may double book these tasks during floor time or an open house, but if you get busy and do not have the chance to accomplish them, it is a good idea to know they are elsewhere on your schedule. If you manage to accomplish them when double booking, you'll have some free time that you can spend any way you wish. You may want to make additional phone calls, take a client to lunch, or just go sit in the park with a good book.

### Handling Paperwork

Create a calendar for every transaction so that you know what needs to be accomplished and when. Put those tasks on your to-do list and on your master calendar. Block out time to accomplish the items on the list, such as ordering inspections and coordinating with the lender.

As your business increases, paperwork increases. Some transactions can become quite complicated, but even "simple" transactions require attention and care to make it to closing. You will find this method very helpful to keep things from slipping through the cracks. Your clients will see your competence and appreciate the attention. That could mean referrals for you.

## Alert

If you have a transaction coordinator in your office you may not need to block out time to accomplish paperwork, but you may still want to check in with the transaction coordinator once a week or so to be sure everything is on track.

### Continuing Education

Although their requirements differ, more and more states are increasing the amount of time you need in continuing-education credits. Block out time each month to take one or two classes. This way, you won't be scrambling to take everything that is required in a few weeks, or worse, a few days, as your license comes due.

You can also block out time for continuing education that has a value to you, other than license credits. You may want to take up a foreign language to help with potential clients who may otherwise be missed. You may want to take a personal marketing class or a seminar about a local project that is under way (such as a new shopping mall being built). In other words, don't limit your classes to those that give you continuing-education credits, but don't neglect the requirements of your state either.

### The Ringing Phone

A natural concern about building your business could lead you to answer every phone call as it comes in, but that can sometimes be inefficient. If you have nothing to do, or you are just addressing envelopes or putting stamps on postcards, it's okay to take every phone call. However, if you are in the middle of something important or complicated, it may be unwise to answer the phone and derail your train of thought. Shifting gears too often can cause you to lose focus—and you can't afford a breakdown.

Do some time-blocking with your calls so that the ringing phone does not rule your time. Time-blocking means that you return calls during a certain period of time. It helps if you change the outgoing message on your voice mail every day. For example: "Hi, this is Annie Agent. It is Monday the fourth and I will be showing property part of the day. I will be returning calls between eleven and twelve and again between four and five. Please leave your name and a number where you can be reached during those hours. I look forward to speaking with you." This message gives callers a sketch of your schedule for the day, and an idea of when they can expect to hear from you.

**Essential**

Tell the person who answers the phone at the office your program for returning calls. Request that all calls go to voice mail unless you request otherwise. This will eliminate being constantly interrupted.

## *Monkey Wrenches*

Time-blocking is important but real estate does not always work exactly as planned. If something needs to be accomplished immediately, you will have to be flexible. What if someone wants to write an offer? Make a few calls, cancel what you need to cancel, and write the offer! Some monkey wrenches are just what we are hoping for and some are a disaster. If you get a call that a window has been broken at one of your vacant listings, you'll need to drop everything for that, too. Gauge what is urgent and what can wait as you deal with the unexpected.

Remember that you are still a real estate professional everywhere you go. You could well meet your next client in the grocery store or at the beauty salon. So, don't worry that maintaining your life will cut into your business. On all levels, a properly maintained life can only help your business, and isn't having a good life part of why you went into real estate in the first place?

Chapter 6

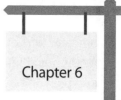

# Working with Other Real Estate Professionals

**A single real** estate agent performs only one portion of the tasks necessary to secure a transaction and get it to closing. Making the transaction a trouble-free experience for buyers and sellers takes a combined effort from a larger team of real estate professionals. You can help ensure that your clients are happy during and after the sale by finding and working with a network of competent, ethical professionals.

## *Build a Support System*

Your clients will nearly always ask you to recommend the additional real estate professionals they'll need to complete their transaction. The list of people they might need to work with includes bank loan officers or mortgage brokers, attorneys, title companies, home and pest inspectors, appraisers, land surveyors, repair services, general contractors, and anyone else who takes part in the steps required to buy or sell real estate. Start identifying the best individuals for specific situations now so that you can make recommendations to your clients when they ask for your advice.

Always try to give your clients choices by offering at least two contact names for each type of service—three is better. Sending your buyers and sellers to any one individual could have negative repercussions for you if the client has problems with the services provided—even if it's simply a personality conflict. Leave the final choice of service providers up to your clients.

Unless they've bought and sold a great deal of real estate themselves, new agents don't always have a lot of firsthand experience with the supporting professionals who are involved in a sale. If you aren't sure where to start, begin by talking to the other agents in your office to find out which members of the real estate community they recommend for certain tasks. Visit your local Chamber of Commerce and pick up business cards and brochures for area service providers. Check the roster of your local Board of Realtors®. Real estate professionals in related fields are often affiliate members.

Firsthand knowledge of how each person handles transactions is something you'll acquire over time as you see them complete their jobs. For now, call or visit with as many service providers as possible to introduce yourself and start forming opinions about their personalities and the way they handle questions.

**Fact**

The word *steering* usually describes an illegal practice that takes place when minority homebuyers are shown only properties within a certain geographic area. The term can also be used to describe agents who steer their clients to specific real estate professionals—and who sometimes receive illegal compensation for doing so. Giving your clients choices helps you avoid accusations of steering.

### Bank Loan Officers vs. Mortgage Brokers

Loan officers working at a bank or savings and loan company are employees of that single lender and can offer your clients its loan products. Mortgage brokers are independent agents who often network with hundreds of lenders throughout the country, including lenders who will approve loans for people with blemished credit or people who have been self-employed for a short time. These are loans that individual banks often have a more difficult time achieving, such as loans for those with less than perfect credit, but individual banks often have great programs for people with excellent credit and regular employment histories. Get to know your local loan officers and mortgage brokers so that you can suggest an appropriate mortgage solution that suits the needs of your buying clients.

### Follow Through

Your task is to find service providers who care deeply about customer service. Think about the typical real estate closing and the relatively short amount of time you have to complete the transaction—sometimes as little as thirty days. Every provider your client chooses must be someone you can depend on to complete her share of the work competently and on time. Delays lead to frustration and frustration often leads to abandoned contracts. That is not good for your career or your client's peace of mind.

**Essential**

Your firm might already have a contact list that has been compiled for agent use. Go with the standard list until you feel confident enough to make additions or other changes that reflect your own opinions.

Being able to give your clients a thoughtful, honest opinion about service providers is an ability you'll develop over time. Ask your broker-in-charge for advice if you don't feel you can develop a list of real estate professionals yourself.

## *Teaming Up*

More agents are switching to the team system every year, working with another agent to share duties and responsibilities and splitting the earnings that are a result of their combined efforts. There are pros and cons to working as a team. Evaluate your goals and unique situation before making a commitment to work with another real estate agent.

You and your teammate can negotiate any percentage split that suits you both. Agents working on a true team usually share their commission income equally, because workload is shared equally. Anything less than an equal split of duties might be better handled by making the person who contributes less to the effort a part-time assistant instead of a teammate.

You don't have to be best friends with your teammate but it is important that you share common goals. Are you both full-time agents? If not, do you both normally work approximately the same number of hours? If the number of hours you can work isn't comparable with your teammate's, wait a bit before joining forces. There is sure to be resentment if one of you isn't handling a fair share of the load.

### Fact

Two-agent teams are common but a real estate team can be made up of more agents, if that suits the goals of its members. Try participating in a two-agent team first to see if the team concept works for you. The two of you can add more members later.

Does your proposed teammate share your ideals for customer service? Do you like the way she interacts with clients? Do you trust her ability to negotiate offers and contracts? Would you be comfortable going on vacation and turning your clients over to her? If you answered "no" to any of those questions, you should probably keep searching for a more suitable teammate. The person you choose must be someone you would trust to handle any portion of your workload.

## Why Work as a Team?

Some real estate agents are more productive working with a teammate than they are when working alone. Perhaps you can handle every aspect of the job but you prefer to focus on paperwork and scheduling, while your teammate is a people-person who loves to work with clients. That scenario could produce the perfect team because it would allow each of you to excel in your own niche.

You've heard the old saying, "Two heads are better than one." It's absolutely true in real estate. Every person brings her own ideas and expertise to the team. Sharing ideas about marketing methods and ways to work effectively with clients is often enough to trigger solutions that help you both. Teammates share expenses too, so a portion of your advertising costs and other expenses will drop if you team up with someone.

### E Alert

Some agents are concerned that as part of a team, they'll share all of their commissions with another person. That's not always an issue. Two working agents will likely generate more than twice as much income as one person. They may generate more by encouraging each other and working together to find methods to increase their business.

## A Written Agreement

Your real estate firm probably requires all team members to sign a written agreement that dictates how commissions are paid when any member closes a transaction. You can draft a simple agreement yourselves or ask an attorney to do it for you.

Team members often sign a more detailed document for each other, describing the team's entire agreement. It might include:

- How commissions are shared
- How clients are distributed among team members
- Expectations for average hours worked, vacation time, etc.
- How expenses are shared

No two agreements are alike. Personalize yours to meet the needs of your team.

## If You Need a Little Help

Some people work better alone. You may fall into that category, but it's a given that there will be times you need help from another real estate agent. You might already be booked solid with appointments when a client calls and asks to look at homes or your vacation is coming up and an out-of-town prospect is flying in on short notice. No matter what the reason, it's nice to have another agent (or two) who can be called on to help when you can't be there.

Agreements between agents who only occasionally share duties are varied. You might decide to help each other out on an as-needed basis, with no money changing hands, or you can agree to share a portion of your commission if and when the client closes on a property, with the percentage determined by the level of help you receive. Put your agreements in writing so that you each understand how you will be compensated when you work with another agent's clients. Sometimes this is outlined in your office's policies and procedures manual, so be sure you are not doing anything that is against company policy.

### Don't Do Everything Together

It doesn't make much sense to work in a team if you do everything together. Two people showing properties to different clients can generate two contracts—show together and a single contract is what you can expect. Each agent should be able to take over the other's tasks if necessary, but you can work more effectively if each team member is primarily responsible for achieving tasks that suit her expertise—whether it's paperwork and advertising or dealing one-on-one with clients and other agents.

It's sometimes helpful if both team members are present for listing presentations to help answer questions, offer support, and to make sure the client is aware that he has two agents working for him instead of one. There may also be times you feel uncomfortable working with a client you don't know very well. Don't hesitate to ask your teammate to accompany you if having another person present makes you feel safer.

### Family Teams

The family team has become more and more common, usually a husband and wife, who work well together and complement each other's strengths. This can be a beneficial pairing, because you are already quite familiar and are working toward the same goals. You and your spouse may work well together. Perhaps you had another business before you got into real estate and know you will be comfortable. Even so, you will need to adhere to a few rules to keep your marriage and your real estate business intact: Don't bring the work home with you, and don't argue in front of clients.

**E Alert**

An aspect to consider about pairing up with a spouse is that husband and wife teams need a backup for vacations. Other family arrangements, such as a father-daughter team or a team of brothers, can sometimes take over each other's job when one of them isn't there.

Although it can take place in all teams, one of the stresses of family teams is "who is the boss?" If the wife was a real estate agent for a number of years and her husband joins her at retirement, she may consider him a novice and want to create a set of rules for everything he does. On the other hand, if a group of siblings decides to be a team, even if they start at the same time, it is common for the eldest to think of himself as the boss. Be sure to outline how your family team dynamic is run, just as if you were not family members.

## Working Alone

Some agents prefer to work alone. Knowing that you are ultimately responsible for your success or failure can be appealing to a person who usually chooses to work alone. An agent working alone does not have to worry if her teammate is doing his fair share; she knows that she is doing it all. Agents who work alone generally enjoy being in control of the transaction and knowing what the steps are from start to finish. They are not unhappy doing it all, but instead may even like the process.

A lone agent can still be very successful, especially if he surrounds himself with others who can aid in that success. Backup agents and assistants, other real estate professionals, and even building a team of agents beneath you (where you are the head of the team and the team members are your employees) will give you the benefits of the team and the autonomy of working alone.

## *Hiring an Assistant*

Whether you work alone or on a team, most successful real estate agents eventually need administrative help. The solution is to hire an assistant. Choose someone with a real estate license if you want an assistant who can show properties, write advertising copy, explain contracts, and help out with other tasks that an agent would perform. State laws restrict the type of work an unlicensed assistant can do, usually limiting it to clerical duties. Your local MLS might limit an unlicensed assistant even more by denying him access to its database for even simple tasks such as printing out copies of listings for you.

**Fact**

An unlicensed assistant can usually relay some details to customers, passing on the same type of information that is seen in your printed ads. He cannot take part in detailed discussions about the pros or cons of listed properties. In most states, an unlicensed assistant cannot quote the listing price, even if the price is advertised.

Most agents feel that a licensed agent is the best choice when it's time to choose an assistant, because they can assist with more tasks. Many agents, however, are satisfied with hiring an unlicensed assistant. Remember that a licensed assistant may one day be your competition, so choose carefully.

### Independent Contractor or Employee?

Licensed real estate assistants are usually independent contractors, often called IC, a status that allows you to pay your assistant lump sums of money as agreed, with all taxes due for the income the responsibility of the assistant. If your assistant is not licensed, it is generally best to hire her as an employee. In this case, you will be responsible for deducting and submitting federal and state taxes from her paycheck—and paying more taxes and benefits on her behalf in addition to her salary.

## Essential

The Internal Revenue Service's Web site, *www.irs.gov.*, is an excellent source of up-to-date guidelines regarding who is and is not considered an independent contractor.

If your assistant is an independent contractor, you and your assistant should sign a written agreement that states this fact. Keep in mind that the whole concept of IC does give the person more independence than an employee has. You can and should agree on the IC's job description, but you can't direct exactly where or how the tasks will be completed. Talk to a local accountant or tax attorney to help devise an agreement that accomplishes what you need while staying within the IC guidelines.

As an option, you may wish to hire all licensed and non-licensed assistants as employees. Their employee status will give you more control over how they perform tasks for you.

### Assistant's Job Description

You'll have a better feel for the type of assistant you need if you take some time to write a detailed job description. What tasks would you like to eliminate from your own daily chores in order to make your life easier and increase your business at the same time?

- Compiling contact information about local for sale by owners
- Making daily phone calls to service providers to track closing status
- Scheduling showing appointments for buyers and listed properties
- Getting verbal or written feedback from agents who show your listings

- Writing advertising copy and submitting it to publications on time
- Updating your Web site and answering e-mails

The list of tasks an assistant will handle helps you pinpoint the type of individual who will best fill the role.

If you have an administrative assistant, one who is not licensed, you may also put him in charge of personal items for you, such as picking up your dry cleaning or having your car serviced. As long as these things are in your assistant's job description, having someone take care of the mundane tasks can free you up to have more face-to-face time with clients.

**Fact**

The Internet is growing more important for real estate advertising each year. Computers and related digital equipment, such as cameras and scanners, are essential for use locally and to make sure you can correspond with potential clients by e-mail. If possible, find an assistant who is already computer savvy.

### The Assistant's Workplace

Some assistants work from their home offices, but you might find that your assistant is more helpful if he accomplishes his tasks at your office, because that is the place clients associate with you. Location can affect IC status, so run the scenario by your accountant to make sure you are staying within the guidelines.

You may be limited by the guidelines your firm has in place for hiring assistants. Is there room for your assistant within your workspace? Who will provide your assistant's desk and other equipment? It's best for someone working as an IC to provide as much of his own equipment as possible.

If you are producing the commissions of two average agents in your office, you should not have difficulty requesting an additional desk for your assistant. Most offices are supportive of agents who are growing and expanding their business and will do what they can to accommodate you. If your assistant does work from the office, even if she is not licensed, you will need to be sure that she abides by the office dress code and other rules of conduct expected of the agents.

### Where to Find an Assistant

Contact a prelicensing school and ask to give a short presentation right before class starts or just after a break. Take a few minutes to introduce yourself and tell the group you are looking for a licensed assistant. Leave single-page flyers at the school that contain a basic job description and your brief bio. Staple a business card to each flyer so that interested students can find you easily.

Is there a new agent in your office who seems ethical and competent but whose business isn't taking off rapidly? That person might welcome the opportunity to be an assistant for a busy, successful agent who can teach her the businesses as she performs her job. You might lose that type of assistant eventually if they become confident enough to go it alone, but life is all about change. Agents talk. Having been a caring mentor for a new agent, instead of simply a boss, nearly always helps you when you search for a new assistant.

## *Networking with Other Agents*

The other agents in your area are your competitors, and you'll find that some will be more open to a cordial working arrangement than others. It's sad, but a small percentage of agents even regard new agents as interlopers—people whose very presence diminishes their own income potential. You'll work with all kinds of people and it won't take long to determine which agents make a transaction easier to complete than others.

## Fact

Your willingness to work honestly and cordially with other agents can help your business. Consider two similar homes: Which would you rather show your buyer, the listing held by an agent who isn't cooperative with others or the listing held by an agent who does everything possible to answer questions and get contracts to closing?

Attend your local MLS functions and take part in its activities. Volunteer to serve on committees and run for office when you feel you can work those tasks into your schedule. Be supportive of other agents and treat them as coworkers—not competitors. Show the real estate community that you are a person who will work with them to do what is best for their interests as well as yours.

Knowing other agents will make you more comfortable when you want to pick up the phone or e-mail them about a new listing. If you need to ask questions about another agent's properties, it is always easier to ask someone with whom you have a relationship. Be cordial and helpful. Do your share of the work. Your reward will be an increase in business for your own listings.

## Agent-to-Agent Ethics

Your local real estate MLS or board office will probably schedule you for an orientation class as soon as you become affiliated with one of its member offices. They'll teach you to use the MLS system and will make you aware of local real estate customs. One of the most important topics your board office will discuss is ethics and how it applies to working with the public and with other agents.

Realtors® are expected to abide by the organization's formal Code of Ethics. If your local real estate board is affiliated with the National Association of Realtors®, you must follow its code to remain a member in good standing and you must take periodic educational updates to remind you of code guidelines and changes. You can read the Realtor Code of Ethics at the NAR's Web site, *www.realtor.org*.

The agents in your own town won't offer you referrals, but there are plenty of distant agents out there who will. Take plenty of business cards with you when you attend educational classes or real estate expos in other towns. Interact with other agents. Hand out your cards and ask others for theirs. Ask them to send you referrals when they have clients relocating to your area. Offer to do the same for them. Keep in touch with these agents on a regular basis. A few weeks after a seminar, your business card will be lost in the sea of others if you don't stay in touch. You probably won't pick up a great many referrals at first but, over time, your networking will definitely increase your business. Keep at it and never miss a chance to introduce yourself!

Chapter 7

# Your Sphere of Influence

**Your sphere of** influence is the single greatest tool you have for creating a thriving business as a real estate agent. People you know are the people most likely to work with you. They are also the people most likely to refer you to their friends and family. Start building your business by working within your sphere of influence and cultivating those relationships. Nothing will grow your business faster than working with people who already trust and believe in you.

## *What Is a Sphere of Influence?*

A sphere of influence is a list of people comprised of everyone you know and everyone who knows you. You encounter them everywhere you go, including work, school, in neighborhoods, through clubs and organizations, out shopping, doing errands, attending parties, and at a religious institution. Your sphere of influence is made up of the people with whom you interact throughout your life. It includes your family, close and distant friends, and people you know but with whom you are not well acquainted. If you work your sphere of influence aggressively, the people in it can help jump-start your career as they pass along information within their own spheres, sharing with their acquaintances and families that you can help them buy or sell real estate.

It is generally believed that the average adult knows about 400 people by name, and knows them well enough to have a conversation with them. This means that your immediate sphere includes about 400 people. If each person in your sphere of influence has a sphere of 400 people, the next sphere level contains 160,000 people! This means you have the chance of working with tens of thousands of people, not just the people in your sphere but also the people in their spheres.

## *Identifying Your Sphere of Influence*

To discover who will most likely be in your sphere of influence, spend some time brainstorming and make a list of everyone you know. Your family members and friends come first. Even include people you think may be the obvious, such as your mom and your cousins. Work your way through the people you know, from people you meet at school or the gym to colleagues from previous and current jobs and even the person who runs the dry cleaner. If you have already developed some client or customer relationships, place them in your sphere as well.

**Essential**

> The best results from brainstorming come when you let the names flow without stopping to eliminate anyone. You may eliminate people later, but putting everyone on the list keeps the brainstorming process moving.

Your holiday card list is a great place to start when compiling your list, and you can expand from there. It is easier to remember everyone you need or want to remember if you create a group of lists. Your groups may look something like this:

- Parents
- Siblings
- Aunts and uncles
- Cousins
- Nieces and nephews
- Grandparents
- Spouse's relatives
- Friends
- Acquaintances
- Previous work colleagues
- Owners and employees of the businesses you frequent

- School (look through the yearbooks)
- Religious organization
- Parents of your kid's friends
- PTA
- Neighbors
- Service clubs and organizations
- Gym or athletic pursuits (such as a bowling league or golf club)
- Veterans group

Continue to add to the lists as you think of people. If you have an address, phone number, and e-mail address for anyone, add those too.

Once you have created a list of everyone, you will want to prioritize the list:

1. People you are comfortable calling and asking for their business.
2. People you are comfortable calling but are not ready to ask for their business.
3. People you are not ready to call but are comfortable writing to.
4. People you don't want to talk to or write to.

## Putting Your Sphere into Action

The saddest sentence a new agent can hear is "I would have used you as my agent but I didn't know you had a license, so I used someone else." Don't assume that everyone you know will be seeking you out when they need a real estate agent. Even if you tell people that you have your real estate license, it may not be enough information for them to know they should send you business. You need to let them know you are a real estate agent, ask them to work with you, and ask them for referrals of their friends and family.

## Fact

Not everyone will jump at the chance to use you as a real estate agent. Some people will already know of an agent, and others will be concerned that you are too inexperienced. Do not take this rejection personally.

Go back to your priority categories, one through four, and decide if there are any people in category four you would like to work with. If so, place them in category three and eliminate all the rest of the names in category four. Remember, those names were only on the list to keep the brainstorm juices flowing. There is no point in spending energy on people with whom you don't want to work.

The way you contact the people within your sphere of influence is as varied as the types of people who are in it. You probably talk with your family members and close friends regularly, so they should already know that you are a new real estate agent. Be sure they also know you want their referrals. There are others on the list whom you see only occasionally. Your relationships with people in that category dictate the best approach to take to tell them about your new career.

## Alert

People you don't want to work with would probably not choose to work with you either. Because you do not like them, even if they did want to work with you, you might find it difficult to do business with them. Don't waste your time convincing people you don't like that you are the real estate agent they should use.

Call people you know and follow up each phone call with a short letter that tells them how to contact you. Be sure to include your business card. Make it a priority to write to acquaintances on your list or to hand out business cards to them the next time you see them at club meetings and other events. Knock on your neighbors' doors and give them your card. Talk or write to every person on your list and add names to the list as you meet new people.

Send an announcement to let everyone in your sphere of influence know that you are now a real estate agent. This announcement should include your picture, your name, your office name, and your contact information. It should tell your sphere of influence what you can do for them, ask for their business, and also ask them to send you referrals to their friends and family. Mail the postcard out to everyone on priority lists one, two, and three.

An example may look something like this:

> Angelina Agent brings ten years of experience in sales and marketing to help you buy and sell property. If you or anyone you know is interested in buying, selling, or investing in real estate, contact Angelina today, 555-1234, or e-mail to *angelina@realestateeasy.com.*

Or this:

> Peter Agent uses his twenty years as a contractor to show you the potential in every house. If you or anyone you know is interested in buying, selling, or investing in real estate, contact Peter today, 555-4321, or e-mail to *peter@sellandbuytoday.com.*

One week after mailing the announcement, call everyone on priority list one. Ask them if they got the announcement. Ask them if they know anyone interested in buying or selling real estate at this time. If they say yes, ask them for permission to contact the people they know. Request that they call first to get permission. You don't want to get in trouble with the National Do Not Call Registry.

## E Alert

The penalties for calling people who are registered with the Do Not Call list are very high. To keep from being penalized, it is wise to register with the National Do Not Call Registry at *https://telemarketing.donotcall.gov* for a continually updated list of registered telephone numbers.

When you contact the prospect, ask if you can do anything for them, such as a free market analysis. Next, call everyone on priority list two. Ask if they got the announcement and ask if there is anything you can do for them. If you are comfortable asking for business, do so now. If not, you may wait until your second mailing.

If you can call the people on priority list three, perhaps they belong in category two. If not, wait until later.

One month after the first mailing, send out a second mailing. It can be the exact same announcement or it can be a little different. If you have already gotten some business, you may want to toot your own horn, like this:

> Just Listed! Angelina Agent has just listed 1234 Grove Street for $185,000. Darling three-bedroom chalet. Contact Angelina if you or anyone you know may be interested in this chalet or in other real estate. 555-9876 or *www.angelinarealestate.com.*

Or this:

> Just Sold! Peter Agent represented the buyers on the sale of 567 Main Street and they are planning a remodel, thanks to Peter's ideas! Contact Peter if you or anyone you know may be interested in seeing the potential in property that may otherwise be missed. 555-5432 or *www.peterrealestate.com.*

After this mailer goes out, follow up with phone calls, asking if they received the mailer and asking for business. If you are consistent with your mailers and calls, you will see results. Be patient, though; it may take some time.

Once you have developed a system of mailing and calling, you will want to start a newsletter or a neighborhood bulletin. There are companies available that will even write your newsletters and personalize them for you. This is a great option if you feel that writing a newsletter is beyond your comfort level. There are also marketing companies who will create monthly postcards with your name, address, phone number, and photograph, as well as a small bit of interesting information.

Postcards are great when you are on a budget. They are less expensive to mail and they usually get read, because opening an envelope is not required. Recipe cards, schedules for local sports teams, or reminders such as the day to change your clocks for daylight savings time are simple ideas of things to put on postcards or magnets that are often saved by the recipient.

## The Importance of Referrals

We ask for referrals for restaurants, movies, a hairdresser, a doctor, or a plumber. When we are in need of virtually anything, from professional services to a great vacation spot, chances are we first seek a referral from someone we trust. When people look for a real estate agent, they are likely to ask someone they trust for a referral.

When you first start in the business, you may get a referral just because you are a great person. Once you have some experience, referrals come from the type of service you provide. Providing exceptional service will help you reap the benefits of referrals. If you only provide satisfactory or less than satisfactory service, don't expect people to recommend you.

**Essential**

When you receive a referral from someone within your sphere of influence, it is critical that you acknowledge that referral right away—with a token of appreciation or a thank-you note. Even if some of the referrals don't buy or sell, you want your sphere to know that sending you referrals is appreciated.

When someone's friend or colleague needs an agent, you want to be the agent that people refer. In order to be that agent, you must constantly ask for referrals. Agents who have built their business by referral have elevated asking for referrals to an art form. These agents don't just expect their friends and family to hand out business cards. Handing out business cards is great but it is not enough. In order to get referrals, it is important that your friends and family get permission for you to contact the people they are referring; they need to get their contact information and pass it to you. When someone receives a business card there is a small chance that he or she will call you. When they give out their name and number for you to contact them, you know that you have a real lead.

## Expanding Your Sphere of Influence

Getting to know more people will help you expand your sphere of influence. Join a club or organization, participate in community activities, join the Chamber of Commerce, or donate time to a local charity—all of these things will help to expand your sphere.

Following is a list of some organizations, clubs, and activities that you could get involved with as a volunteer. Use this list as a starting place to discover where you want to spend your volunteer hours. This is not a complete list; there are thousands of opportunities nationwide. Most communities also have their own local charities that are not available anywhere else. Look for something that interests you, decide how much time you are willing to devote, and start getting involved.

- Chambers of Commerce
- American Association of University Women (AAUW)
- Local politics
- Board of Realtors®
- The American Legion
- American Veterans (AMVETS)
- Fraternal Order of Eagles
- Benevolent and Protective Organization of Elks of the USA
- Junior Chamber of Commerce (Jaycees)
- Kiwanis International
- Knights of Columbus
- Lions Club International
- Loyal Order of Moose
- Optimist International
- Rotary International
- Veterans of Foreign Wars (VFW)
- Art society
- Music society
- Bridge club
- Book club
- Historical society
- Zoo
- Museum docent
- PTA
- College
- Volunteering at the school
- Scouting
- Boys and girls clubs
- Hospital volunteer
- American Red Cross
- Fire department
- Family services
- Crisis line
- Food bank
- Food kitchen
- Salvation Army

- United Way
- Library volunteer
- MOMS Club
- Humane Society
- Habitat for Humanity
- Your political party
- Church, temple, or other religious or spiritual practice
- Elderly services
- Disability services
- Literacy program
- Golf club
- Tennis club
- Hiking club
- Biking club
- Sailing club
- Recreation league baseball
- Gym
- Coaching kids in sports
- Booster club

### E Alert

Remember that many service organizations are in great need. It's easy to get caught up in the action and volunteer for more than you can handle. Make a firm time commitment and stick to it. Your time commitment will make it easier to say no if the organization asks for more than you are willing to do.

If you join an organization only to get business, people will realize that and you will be judged as a phony. Join because it is something you believe in or like, and people will know that you are sincere. Start by deciding what interests you. It is okay to let people know you are a real estate agent, but participate in the organization for the fun of it. Wait a while before you actually ask for business, but even if you ask, don't push. Remember, you joined this organization for fun. Once people see your sincerity they will be more comfortable offering you business. It is okay to tell people what you do.

**Essential**

> If you have a local newspaper, you may want to volunteer to write a weekly column. It can be a real estate column, but it does not have to be. Anything from high school sports news to what the local volunteer organizations are doing will still get your name (and hopefully your picture) in the paper every week.

If you are new to a community, it is even more important to expand your sphere of influence by becoming involved. You might even choose to be involved in multiple activities. This will give you a sense of belonging and it will also connect you to a multitude of different people. You may still get referrals from those you knew in your old hometown, but not all of them will be sending business directly to you. Some may have friends who want to move to your new location and some may ask you for a referral to an agent in your old community, now that you are gone. You will have fewer referrals if you fail to reach out to your new community.

Volunteering increases the possibility of receiving referrals, but it can also increase your enjoyment of life. Participating in sports, giving back to your community, helping others, or a combination of these activities will make you a well-rounded individual. Well-rounded people are also better real estate agents.

## The Extra Step

Consistently sending out mailers and making calls is a great way to stay in touch, but there is another way of staying in touch that will have even more impact. It is giving your time. Your time is the most valuable asset you have and it is the most cherished by those who receive it. Giving your time, not only to your volunteer organizations but also to your friends, family, and all the people in your sphere of influence, will do more to bring you referrals than any other activity. Set aside time each week to drop by and visit someone in your sphere at their home or business, bring a small gift such as a gourmet chocolate bar or a seasonal item (Fourth of July flag or Halloween pumpkin), and spend some time just listening to them. Let them know that you are never too busy for them and that you are never too busy for referrals. Not only will your personal contact help grow your business, but it will enrich your life as well.

Chapter 8

# Personal Marketing

**Nearly all real** estate agents are self-employed. Even though the firm you represent might print your photo and contact information in its general ads, you are responsible for planning and paying for nearly all aspects of your own marketing. Your personal marketing campaign will change as you determine which techniques work best for you, but it's critical to implement at least a few marketing strategies from the very first day you go to work.

## *Establishing an Image*

Your personal image is linked, in part, to your dress and appearance. What is proper for one agent doesn't necessarily work for another. As noted earlier, suitable attire varies depending on where you work and the types of properties you work with, so don't assume that a business suit is your best choice. Agents who sell large tracts of land won't be ready to help buyers find property lines if they show up in a suit and tie—casual clothes and hiking boots might be more appropriate. Agents working in a tourist area, where people buy second homes, might opt for dressy-casual clothes. That is likely what their clients will wear when they take advantage of a little vacation time while house hunting.

Your office might have a dress code. If it doesn't, you can get a feel for suitable attire by paying attention to the dress of successful agents in your area. There is no need to mimic them exactly. Develop your own style but try to make it a style that fits in with what is acceptable in your town.

Your attitude is every bit as important to your image as your outward appearance. If you're a new agent, you might be nervous about talking with prospects, especially if you don't feel you can answer all of their questions, and that nervousness is apparent to people. Try to relax and let your self-confidence show. Even if you don't immediately know all of the answers to their questions, customers will have faith in your ability if they see that you are ethical and sincere about helping them. If you don't have the answers but know where to get them, most people will still be happy to work with you.

### Your Business Cards

Your real estate firm might have a predesigned business card for its agents, a template that is set up for each agent to customize with a photo and personal information, such as a cell phone number and e-mail address. If using a photo is optional, always choose the photo card. Everyone you hand the card to is a potential client. You want them to remember your name *and* your face when it's time to buy or sell real estate.

**Essential**

> Be sure that the photo on your card looks like you. An airbrushed photo might make you feel better, but you want people to recognize you from the photo when they see you. Update your picture every few years. You may not think you look different, but chances are your style has changed enough that a current picture is needed.

Some firms allow agents to design their own business cards if certain company guidelines are followed, such as mandatory use of the company logo. Personal card design gives you the opportunity to make sure your name and permanent contact information are the most prominent aspects of the business card. You might choose not to include the firm's phone number, or to include it in small letters. Let's face it—agents don't always stay with the same agency for their entire careers, but people do hang on to old business cards. You want them to find you no matter when they decide to buy or sell, so your permanent contact information is the most important data on your card. Your cell phone number or personal e-mail address will move with you.

### Logos and Mottos

Some agents use a graphic logo or short motto in all of their advertising. This is a design or statement that, after a time, always reminds potential clients of you. Let your photo be your logo, so that people remember your face. You could also choose something that ties in to your work, such as a drawing of your town or your general area. If you use a drawing, keep it simple so that it can be reproduced easily in all types of advertising formats.

**E Alert**

Check with your state for regulations regarding the size of company logos on business cards and other forms of advertising. Some states require that the company information is more prominent, or larger, than your personal information.

Choose a motto that fits your personality or the goals you're trying to achieve in real estate. Read real estate ads nationwide and you'll see mottos ranging from "We buy ugly homes" to "Your hard-working neighbor." Keep your motto short so that it's easy to remember and doesn't overshadow the rest of your advertising copy.

## Make Yourself More Visible

Visibility is an important key to success in real estate, so you should take advantage of every opportunity you can find to promote yourself and the services you offer. It takes a little time and effort, but the good news is that you can increase your visibility without spending a fortune on expensive advertising.

If you don't already take part in local activities, do so! Become active in your community. Volunteer at charitable institutions or thrift stores. Join civic organizations such as your local historical society and take time to participate in their events. Do you have hobbies and special interests? Join a motorcycle club, a photography group, a gem and mineral society—whatever interests you.

You can become a member of your local Chamber of Commerce and participate in its activities, which are often designed to help local businesses network with each other. Set up a booth at street fairs or at other events where you have the opportunity to talk to people and hand out business cards. Analyze your interests and the events that take place in your community to determine which activities are best for you.

## The Press Release

Submit a press release to all local newspapers as soon as you become associated with a real estate firm. Press releases are regarded as news—so they are free—and a great way to notify the public that you are now a real estate agent. People who don't know you might not remember your name after reading the press release, but your acquaintances will indeed note your new career.

### Fact

Radio stations in smaller towns might be willing to share your press release with listeners, but in larger markets it's more difficult to get free press in any form. Your broker-in-charge can probably suggest local news outlets that are good about featuring press releases from agents.

Call the newspapers before you send the release to find out whom to send it to and if they have specific wording or length guidelines that you must follow. Always submit a photo with the release—if space is available, newspapers will probably use it.

Mark the top of the document "Press Release," and include your name and contact phone numbers under that statement. Write the release in paragraph format and try to limit it to no more than three paragraphs. Be sure to include:

- Your name and the name and town of the firm with which you are associated
- Past experience (if it is relevant to your new position)

- Special real estate designations or educational achievements
- A brief biographical statement
- A contact phone number

Be sure to include interesting information as well. If you've lived in the town all your life, say you're an area native and know the area inside and out. If you've received a broker's license, which is more advanced than a salesperson license, be sure to announce that you are a broker associate—or use wording approved by your state or your firm. Promote yourself as much as possible without making the press release sound like an ad.

If you live in a large metropolitan area that has a regional publication, send a press release to the regional paper. Newspapers in larger metropolitan areas receive a lot of press releases, so you may have to work a little harder to get your name in the paper. Set up an appointment with the editor of the business section and personally deliver your press release to her. Ask her how the paper expects your press release to be laid out and when you can expect to see it in print. This effort can give you an extra edge over the numerous other press releases that are submitted.

Many real estate offices have a standard form for a press release. If yours does not, use this example as a starting point and create your own.

**PRESS RELEASE**

Date, city, state—Robert Agent has joined ABC Realty. Robert brings his expertise in sales and marketing, with twenty years experience at Widget Corporation, to the world of real estate.

At Widget, Robert was in charge of training the sales staff for the highest level of productivity and customer satisfaction. In the past three years, Robert has helped increase Widget's sales by over 300 percent and advanced their customer satisfaction ranking

to first in the nation. He received the coveted Silver Statue Award for this effort. Robert is now bringing his customer satisfaction abilities to real estate and has joined the prestigious firm of ABC Realty.
Robert Agent can be reached at the midtown branch of ABC Realty at 123 Ridge Road. 800-555-1212.

Do not expect that your phone will be ringing with calls from potential buyers and sellers from one or two mentions in the newspaper. Having your press release published is a good beginning, but your name and face must appear many places to remind people that you are a real estate agent and available to help them.

## Local Personal Advertising

There's no shortage of places to spend your local advertising dollars, so it's up to you to determine which avenues will yield the best return. The most basic place to advertise is in newspapers, either in the classifieds or in larger display ads that appear throughout the paper. Neighborhoods often have their own newspapers and while they don't reach as many people as citywide publication, the ads do help you target specific communities.

Your MLS might publish a weekly or monthly real estate magazine and there are probably independent publishers who do the same. Ads in those publications are sometimes expensive, but the magazines are a favorite of both homebuyers and sellers, so an eye-catching ad is sure to get good readership.

### Essential

Ask everyone who contacts you how they heard about you. Over time their answers will indicate which types of advertising generate the best results.

Local cable television companies have informational channels that run continuous ads while news or music is played in the background. Another advertising option is radio advertising. Advertising over the radio is affordable in smaller markets, but the cost is often more than the budget of a new agent can handle.

In addition to the standard advertising options of TV, classifieds, and radio, you are also likely to be approached to pay for your name to be on everything from restaurant menus to county maps. Try to be selective. Start out by inserting classified ads in newspapers and display ads in for-sale publications, then add other types of ads as you can afford them.

### Direct Mailings

Direct mailings include postcards, flyers, letters, and other types of written correspondence that you send to potential and past customers and clients, locally or in other areas. The pieces you mail can be queries that ask for listings or they can promote your current listings. Mailings can be educational, relaying general information about home buying and selling, or they can convey your abilities as an agent.

There is disagreement among agents about the value of direct mailings but nearly everyone agrees that if you do direct mailings at all, you must send them consistently and for a period of time before you can expect to see results. Some agents feel results are best when they send out mailings once each month, altering the content for each mailing. And even though it is more time consuming, many people claim to see better results when recipient addresses are written by hand instead of printed on a computer-generated label. Regardless of the method you choose, mailers always get better response when they are followed up with a phone call. Be sure the person you are calling is someone you have had previous contact with, or crosscheck them to be sure they are not on the National Do Not Call Registry.

Another option for local advertising is the use of bulk mailings. The United States Postal Service (USPS) provides bulk mailing at reduced rates if you send identical items to multiple addresses. You'll need a bulk-mailing permit and you must follow the USPS guidelines when you prepare and mail the documents. Many real estate firms pay the annual fees required for bulk-mailing permits to encourage their agents to send regular promotional materials. Ask your broker-in-charge if that benefit is available to you.

## Question

**Where can I find names for my direct-mailing list?**
The people in your sphere of influence should be on your direct-mailing list. You can also ask your local registrar of deeds or tax assessor's office to provide the names and addresses of all people in the area you wish to target. Some title or escrow companies also provide mailing lists.

Send out a regular first-class postcard mailing before you send bulk letters. First-class mail is returned to you with address changes if an address is not valid. That's a service you must pay for when using the bulk mail system. Periodically doing a first-class postcard mailing is a good way to keep your address database current.

### Outdoor Advertising

Billboards might be the first thing you think of when you hear the term *outdoor advertising*, but there are many other, more affordable ways to promote yourself to people as they drive or walk through your town.

Name riders are essential for real estate agents who have listings. These small but visible signs are designed to attach to either the top or bottom of the larger for sale sign provided by real estate firms. A rider typically includes your name and personal phone number printed in large letters, making it more likely that someone who wants to see the property will call you directly.

Listing agents should also consider investing in brochure boxes. These are waterproof containers that are posted at a property for sale and stocked with flyers about that listing. If you use brochure boxes, check them regularly to make sure advertising materials are available.

Some local businesses sell advertising spaces on park benches. Public transit buses usually have spaces on the back and sides where businesses can advertise. You can also turn your own vehicle into an advertising opportunity by ordering a magnetic sign for its side or paying to get personalized lettering on the back window that displays your name, title, and contact information (you could also include a logo or motto for a more unique and noticeable effect). Local high schools and colleges often sell advertising banners for their football and baseball fields. Some grocery stores sell advertising on shopping carts or provide racks for promotional materials.

Pay attention to the outdoor advertising methods used by other agents and businesses in your town and think of ways to adapt them to suit your own needs.

### Special Promotional Products

You've probably been the recipient of promotional products—pens, pencils, refrigerator magnets, calendars—all personalized with someone's ad and contact information. Some real estate agents purchase promotional products for use throughout the year; others choose to send them to clients with year-end holiday greetings.

**Fact**

If you order personalized giveaways, find something that people will use. Passersby at a summertime outdoor event might appreciate a paper fan to cool them off. Clients might use a magnet with important local numbers printed on it, or they might appreciate a good pen. Find something that won't go in the wastebasket as soon as potential clients get home.

Personalized promotions can be quite expensive, so whether or not you use them depends on your budget. It sometimes makes more sense for new agents to spend those dollars for computer equipment that helps them be more productive or for advertising that will be seen by a greater number of people. Analyze your own situation before you jump in. Don't order products that might sit in your desk for several months before finding a home.

Be creative and think about where other real estate agents *are not* advertising, not just where the top producers are getting leads. Your local high school may be happy to sell soft drinks in cups, donated by you, with your name and logo on them. Many sections of highway or local streets around the country are sponsored by people who promise to clean that section every few months or so. Having your sign on the highway and a crew, with your name and logo on the back of their shirts, picking up trash is a community-minded promotional idea.

## Organize a Home-Buying Seminar

One way to increase visibility among homebuyers, especially first timers, is to organize a home-buying seminar. It isn't difficult, but it does require some advance planning and coordination among other members of the real estate community. If your seminar is a success you might even decide to offer it on a regular schedule.

You can hold a seminar in a variety of local meeting spaces. Your bank might have a meeting room that you can use free of charge or for a small fee. Hotels usually have meeting rooms and so do other area businesses. Your local Chamber of Commerce can probably give you some leads on meeting facilities in your area.

Early weekday evenings are usually the best choice for attracting the most buyers, but try to avoid times when you know that a large number of locals are already booked. Steer clear of conflicts with evening church services, sports events, and holiday festivities.

### Essential

Offering snacks and keeping your seminar short enough for people to get home for dinner will make it easier and more appealing for people to try and fit it into their schedules.

Your seminar will be more educational if it offers advice from a variety of people involved in the home-buying process. You could ask local individuals in related professions to come and speak, including:

- A mortgage broker or loan officer
- A title company representative or closing agent
- An appraiser
- A home inspector
- A pest inspection expert
- A land surveyor

It usually isn't difficult to find people to help you present a seminar, because the event gives them the opportunity to promote their businesses.

Look for real estate professionals you trust and who will give a short talk about home-buying procedures in their allied fields. Allow each person to hold a question and answer period, then send them off to staff tables where people can pick up more information or chat with them in person. Talk to as many people as possible and don't forget to bring your own promotional materials.

Advertise your seminar in as many places as possible. Newspaper classifieds are a good choice and some neighborhood flyers offer free ads. As it's an educational seminar, your area newspapers might even print a press release for you.

Tack up notices on bulletin boards in area self-service Laundromats and grocery stores, just two of the many places where you'll find renters who might want to be homeowners. Ask the people who are helping you with the seminar to spread the word. Tell everyone you know the date and time. Ask them to pass it on to potential homebuyers.

Presenting a home-buying seminar is a service you can provide to your community, an event you can be proud of and something that will help your public image and result in more business leads—the perfect combination!

## *Word of Mouth*

The best promotion you can receive is the word of others. If you sold a house to the owner of a small business and she is happy with your service, ask her to keep your business cards on her counter or in a prominent place in the store. If you frequent the local gym, you may want to give your clients and customers from the gym T-shirts with your contact information on them. Give your friends, family members, clients, and customers some of your business cards in a business card holder to hand out when they hear of someone interested in real estate. Ask them to get the contact information of the person they talked to and pass it to you as well.

By being consistent and far-reaching with your personal marketing, more and more people will come to recognize your name and associate it with real estate. When they are looking for an agent, they'll look no further than your next promotional piece!

Chapter 9

# Successful Listing Presentations

**Listings can add** to your income even when you're on vacation, because you get paid when a listing sells, no matter who sells it. You'll begin to acquire potential listing clients once your personal marketing campaigns start to kick in, but do you know how to work effectively with them? Use the strategies in this chapter to build a listing presentation that suits your style and satisfies your clients.

## *Preparing a Comparative Market Analysis*

A comparative market analysis (called a CMA for short) is a property analysis that real estate agents use to help sellers and buyers determine the market value of real estate. A CMA is not an appraisal, but it does contain some of the same types of information that you'll find in an appraisal. While banks will not use a CMA to verify value before approving a loan, experienced real estate agents can often use the report to come very close to the dollar amount a property will ultimately fetch.

CMAs help you put a value on property for both sellers and buyers, so it's important to learn how to prepare the reports as soon as you start working as an agent. Get started by preparing a practice CMA for your own home, then get more experience by compiling CMAs for any homes or land with which you are familiar.

Although the methods differ, nearly all Multiple Listing Services offer their agents the ability to perform CMAs with the same computer software that is used to search for current and sold listings. You'll find that the software is very easy to use. Instructions included with each system will take you step-by-step through the CMA process.

## Question

**What is an appraiser?**

Real estate appraisals are performed by licensed appraisers—individuals who have attended school, passed an exam, and worked a certain number of hours under the supervision of an experienced appraiser to gain the skills required to offer a detailed opinion of property values. Lenders use appraisers to determine the value of homes on which they lend.

Agent CMAs are prepared by comparing the property you wish to price, called the subject property, with three or four similar properties that have sold in the recent past. You must always use the sales price of sold properties when doing a CMA. This is the data that an appraiser will use when a potential buyer is looking for a loan. Property does not sell based on the prices of sold properties alone—supply and demand is also a factor.

You will also need to compare the subject property to other properties that are currently available to see how it stacks up against the competition.

## Fact

Although listed prices are often inflated, they will give you an idea of what buyers see when they are shopping for a property with similar features or in that price range. Using statistics of properties that were unable to sell (called *expired* in real estate jargon) will also help finalize the picture.

Your goal is to calculate an amount that is as close as possible to what a buyer will ultimately pay for the subject property and what it will appraise for if the buyer is obtaining a loan.

The more details you have about the subject property, the easier it is to prepare a CMA. You should know:

- Location and year built
- The total acreage or lot size
- The number of and types of rooms
- Structural details, such as insulated versus single-pane windows, type of heat and air conditioning, size and type of garage, basement, fireplace, etc.
- Facts about components, such as the types of flooring installed
- Overall condition of the structure and its components
- Style

Don't be surprised if you cannot find three properties that match the subject property exactly, but do the best you can to find close comparisons. CMA software allows you to deduct or add dollar amounts for characteristics of comparable properties, to make them more like your subject property.

Your local real estate market will dictate how far back you should search for sold properties. In a quickly changing market, where prices are escalating rapidly, you might choose to use only properties that have sold during the past few months. In a slower market, you can search back over the previous year. Always use the most recent sales possible when compiling a CMA. Make adjustments on the comparable properties that are currently available and the expired properties as well. All three of these will help you further determine the value.

In a rising market the supply and demand factor will make listing prices more important. In a steady market, it is the sold prices that will be given the most weight. In a falling market, it may actually be the expired properties that show what the trends are and how much the subject property is actually worth.

The ability to compile an accurate CMA for clients is a skill you will develop over time. You will find that the task is much easier when you can make comparisons from firsthand experience rather than through reading a list of features printed on an MLS sheet. Keep up to date with listings by showing them to buyers, previewing them yourself, and by attending every open house you possibly can. When it's time to do a CMA you'll recall those listings and be in a better position to judge exactly how similar they are to your subject.

### E Alert

Your state real estate laws might require you to insert a statement within your CMA that confirms it is a comparative market analysis and not a certified appraisal. States that require that type of disclosure furnish agents with the specific wording to be used.

## Developing Your Listing Presentation

Your first listing clients will most likely come from within your sphere of influence. They will likely be either people you know or people who have heard about you from friends, family, and acquaintances. Your family members might list with you no matter how you present your skills and qualifications to them, but people who are less connected with you will expect you to show them why they should choose you as their listing agent. Start developing your listing presentation as soon as possible and refine it as you learn which aspects of it consumers respond to best.

Tell your broker-in-charge and other agents in your office that you would like to go along with them to listing appointments. Real estate is a competitive business, so you'll find that many agents won't be willing to share their techniques with you, but some will. Every bit of experience you can get will help you develop your own presentation skills. An offer to help take square footage measurements or assist in other ways might be better received than a request to simply tag along. Be creative—think of ways you can be a genuine help to the other agent.

Pay close attention to property owners as the agent makes her presentation and stay alert during your own presentations to recognize how people react. Are there elements of the presentation that seem to turn off sellers completely? Do they become bored and distracted during certain discussions? Which topics interest them the most? Every listing presentation you take part in makes you aware of the things you should—and should not—do when talking to property owners.

## Essential

If you go on a listing presentation with another agent, do not make comments. The agent has the right to work her presentation the way she sees fit. Have the other agent introduce you as someone she is training and, if you are asked a direct question, state that you do not yet have the experience to answer.

Your listing presentation will change as you gain experience and work with enough clients to get a feel for what works best in your area. You'll also discover that a presentation that one client likes won't impress another. Start with the basics and tweak your presentation and handouts until you find a combination that works for you.

Essential presentation items include:

- Your marketing strategy for the property
- A sample listing agreement and property disclosure
- A sample offer to purchase form
- Copies of forms and brochures required by law in your area, such as lead paint information for homes built prior to 1978
- A copy of one of your marketing brochures or a mock-up brochure for that property
- A short biographical sketch of yourself and your firm
- An estimated closing statement

Today's affordable computer systems, digital cameras, and color printers make it possible for you to produce colorful, high-quality handouts for *every* potential listing client, instead of reserving that type of package for high-end properties, as was common in the past. If your office doesn't supply equipment for agent use, invest in the equipment you need as soon as you can afford it. It will add a professional touch to your presentation, and it will reflect the effort you have put in for your clients.

Prepare a CMA ahead of time, but don't present it until you've established a rapport with the sellers. If you prepared it with sketchy knowledge of the property, the pricing might need to be adjusted. Showing it to the sellers before they are acquainted with you could be an immediate turnoff.

**E Alert**

One of the biggest mistakes that even experienced agents make is taking too long to give a listing presentation. You shouldn't move through it so quickly that people can't keep up with what you're saying, but don't get so bogged down in details that you lose their interest halfway through the presentation.

Make changes to the CMA with the sellers by your side (the best solution if you have sellers who want to list immediately) or ask to return again after you've had a chance to update the report (an alternative that keeps you in the minds of sellers who are interviewing other agents).

## *Can They Afford to Sell?*

Before taking a listing, an ethical real estate agent attempts to qualify a seller who plans to sell one property in order to buy another. Determine a price range for the new real estate based on the seller's wants and needs. If the property is in another area, make sure the seller has researched real estate costs at that location.

Ask the seller for his approximate mortgage payoff for the existing property. Deduct the mortgage payoff and an estimate of all selling expenses from the value determined in your CMA to determine how much cash the seller should have left after closing on the property you plan to list.

## Question

**What should I do if the seller won't disclose his payoff amount?** Many sellers do not like to disclose financial information until you are their listing agent. If you cannot determine a payoff amount, estimate other closing expenses and let sellers deduct their payoff from the total after you have left.

Are the proceeds expected from closing enough of a down payment to buy the new property? Has the seller talked to a bank to verify that he qualifies for the new mortgage? Sellers appreciate agents who take this extra step and often reward them with plenty of referrals to family and friends.

Sellers are all different, but you'll find that agent experience is not usually their top priority. They are looking for a real estate agent who listens to them, is personable, explains exactly how their property will be marketed, and who is not evasive when they ask questions. Relax, be yourself, and you'll find that people will give you a chance to represent them.

## *Are They* Really *Ready to Sell?*

Anyone who is thinking of selling a home or other property is a potential client, but many people begin to explore their sales options well in advance of the time they actually intend to sell. You should definitely take time to talk with people who are undecided, and stay in touch with them until they are ready to put a property on the market—but devote the most time to people who wish to sell now.

A ten- or fifteen-minute friendly conversation is usually all it takes to determine if a property owner is ready to sell. Jot down a few important questions and keep them handy so you can pull them out any time a potential listing client comes your way. After a few sessions you won't need your list anymore—you'll know exactly what to ask to determine how serious a person is about selling.

Important questions include:

**1.** Are you ready to sell your property now?

A "no" answer tells you this is someone you should stay in contact with and provide your marketing information. This is probably not a seller you should devote a lot of your in-person time to, until they are closer to their target sell date.

**2.** What events must take place before you sell?

Maybe the owner is waiting for a job promotion or relocation. Perhaps he won't sell until updates or repairs are completed. The answer to this question will help you determine timing and motivation.

**3.** How long do you think it will take to sell your property?

You'll find that most people don't have a clear understanding of how long it takes to sell a property and get it to closing. This discussion gives you the opportunity to explain area averages and educate the seller about local real estate customs. It could lead to an earlier listing date for sellers who have underestimated the average times.

**4.** Do you know what your property is worth?

Unless they've had a recent appraisal, most people do not know the true value of their real estate. Some owners associate a property's assessed tax value with its market value, but tax value is nearly always much less than the actual sale price of the property. You'll also find that many people think their real estate is worth much more than the facts dictate. A discussion of value is your opportunity to explain appraisals and CMAs. Some people will not disclose their perceived value until they hear from you first. They want to see if your number matches their guess.

**5.** Do you plan to buy another property?

If the answer is "yes," you can certainly help them find it. You can do this either through your own efforts or by referring them to an agent in another area who will pay you a commission for the referral.

All of these questions lead to discussions that focus on the owner's true desire to sell. Whether the individual intends to sell immediately or not, make sure you keep track of all potential clients. Send them your promotional mailer every month or so, or write a personal note. Follow up with a phone call. Your continued success in real estate is all about developing future business, so do all you can to make sure it's your name people remember when it's time to list the property.

It is tempting to tell people that their home is worth more than it actually is in order to have them like you and list their property with you. By doing this you are not doing your clients or yourself a service. They will have a house on the market at an overinflated price and you will have a listing that may not sell. Ask the sellers to consider hiring an agent based on the agent's merits and not on what the agent thinks their house is worth. If they think you are the best agent for the job, they should choose you to represent them, even if another agent gave them an inflated value.

## The National Do Not Call Registry

The Federal Trade Commission (FTC) established a National Do Not Call Registry to help protect the privacy of consumers who wish to eliminate annoying calls from telemarketers. The registry laws do not restrict all types of telemarketer calls, but they do affect unsolicited calls made by real estate agents. Agents who violate "do not call" laws are subject to hefty fines.

Your real estate firm can register for access to the National Do Not Call Registry on the FTC's Web site. Agents can then use the firm's account number and password to view the list in order to determine whom they cannot call.

Some states maintain their own "do not call" lists. You will find that many consumers place their name on one list but not the other, so you should always check both state and federal lists before making an unsolicited call. There are exceptions to the "do not call" rules:

- You may call existing customers and customers you have dealt with during the past eighteen months.
- You can make return calls to people who call you, and you can contact those consumers for three months after the initial call.
- You are allowed to call consumers who have granted you written permission to do so.

## Question

**My state no-call laws are more lenient than the federal laws. Which must I follow?**

When laws differ, you should conform your business practices to the laws that are most restrictive. In this case, follow the federal guidelines.

### Calling FSBO and Expired Listings

You cannot call a "for sale by owner" seller whose name is on the list if you are calling to solicit your services as a real estate listing agent. You can call the seller if you are a buyer's agent working with a client who you think would have an interest in the property. Your conversation with the seller should revolve only around your buyers and their needs and should not turn into a discussion about your capabilities as a listing agent.

You may also call consumers who previously listed with you, or someone else in your office, for eighteen months after their listing expiration date.

### Open House Visitors and Referrals

Agents always ask for contact information from guests who visit their open houses. Insert a "yes" check box next to the phone number column that, when checked, authorizes you to make a follow-up call to the individual. Place a statement on each page that makes it clear that visitors who sign the list are authorizing a call.

Because referrals make up a large share of an agent's business, you definitely want to encourage your clients to send their friends and family to you when they need real estate services, but a phone number passed on to you by a client could belong to someone who is on the "do not call" list. If you don't want to call, get the contact's address and send an introductory letter, asking them to call you and explaining why you cannot call them. If time is a factor, ask your former client to have the new prospect contact you.

## Fact

Most people who are referred to you by their friends and family will not be upset if you call them. If sending a letter seems impersonal, talk to the person giving you the referral to verify that the prospect does indeed want to hear from you, then decide whether or not to simply place the call and introduce yourself.

### Calls Made in Error

The FTC's guidelines prevent you from being fined if you make a call in error to someone on the list. If you are a member of the National Association of Realtors®, you can refer to their Web site at *www.realtor.org* for the most current rules.

## Measuring Square Footage

Many complaints have been filed with real estate licensing commissions in recent years claiming that agents inaccurately reported square footage totals on multiple listing sheets, in ads, and within other advertising materials. Most square footage errors are not the result of an agent's desire to be untruthful; they occur because agents do not know how to take measurements and do the calculations. Become familiar with both tasks so that when you state a square footage total, you know it is accurate.

Some agents no longer advertise the square footage of their properties but your MLS might require you to include total square footage so that the house can be better categorized for searches. Square footage is important to most buyers too, and it can be passed on as an approximate number rather than exact total.

## Essential

Agents who follow standard guidelines and document their measuring procedures and calculations are better equipped to defend their square footage findings if a homebuyer files a complaint after the sale. Keep all drawings and related materials in case you must show how a figure was obtained.

Your state real estate commission might have established guidelines to help its licensed agents measure and calculate square footage. If it hasn't, use the techniques in this chapter, which are based on standards that are widely accepted within the housing industry.

### Only Count Finished Living Areas

The square footage you report must be space that's intended for human occupancy and it must be heated by a conventional and permanent heating system. The area must have walls, floors, and ceilings constructed from materials that are generally regarded as acceptable for interior construction.

## Alert

Never use square footage totals from a tax collector's office, a former MLS sheet describing the property, or from a seller. Do not even depend on blueprints, because changes are sometimes made to a home during construction. Unless your MLS guidelines allow otherwise, always measure the house yourself or hire a licensed appraiser to measure it for you.

One common square footage error involves finished rooms that are accessed through an unfinished area, such as a utility room that you enter by passing through a garage. Any room that is accessed through an unfinished area cannot be counted as finished square footage.

## Measuring the House

You might be surprised to learn that houses are measured from the outside, although it's sometimes necessary to deduct space by measuring the dimensions of interior rooms, then adding space back in to account for wall depth. To get started, collect the tools you need to measure the house:

- Paper and ruler (graph paper is handy)
- A long measuring tape
- Pencils and erasers
- A calculator

Measure the length of one side of the house and round the figure to the nearest inch—or nearest quarter inch for better accuracy. Draw a line on your paper to represent the wall and record its length next to the line. Measure the remaining sides of the house, sketching in the shapes as you go and taking care to record lengths.

The simplest square footage to calculate is that of a square or rectangular house with no garage or other unfinished space. If the house is forty feet long by thirty feet deep, multiply those numbers together to get the total square footage, 1,200 feet.

## Measuring Irregular Spaces

Mistakes sometimes happen when houses are more complex, with unfinished rooms that must be deducted from the total and with finished rooms that cannot be measured outside for some reason.

When you must measure an area from the inside, add four inches to the length of walls that butt against an interior wall and six inches to the length of walls that meet an exterior wall. The additions make the room dimensions more equivalent to its exterior measurement.

### *Rooms with Sloped Ceilings*

Some attic rooms and rooms in chalet and A-frame houses have sloped walls. If you measure the dimensions of that type of room all the way to the point where the slope meets the floor you'll be measuring unusable space. Include only the portion of the room where ceiling height is at least five feet tall. Do not include the room at all if at least one half of its square footage does not have ceilings that are a minimum of seven feet high. (You may want to note the total floor area in the remarks section of the MLS, because this would be an important number when calculating certain things, such as the cost of new carpet.)

#### *Bay Windows*

The square footage occupied by a bay window may be counted if the area has a floor, a ceiling height of at least seven feet, and meets the other criteria necessary to qualify it as finished living space.

#### *Furnace Room*

The furnace, water heater, and other similar utility items are often located in a small room or closetlike area within the house. It may be included in the total square footage.

#### *Hallways and Closets*

Hallways and closets are included in the total square footage if they are a functional part of the living space.

#### *Stairways*

If the upper opening for a stairway is larger than its area on the floor below, you should deduct the excess open space from the upper level's square footage.

### Calculations for Specific Shapes

Most of your square footage calculations will be for squares and rectangles, but sometimes other shapes emerge as you sketch the house, such as circular areas for a bay window.

For squares and rectangles, multiply length times width to find the number of square feet. To calculate the area of a triangle, multiply the length of its base by its height and divide the result by two. Calculate the area of a circle by squaring its radius (multiplying it by itself) and multiplying the figure by 3.14. Determine the area of an octagon by first drawing lines to turn it into a rectangle and triangles, then calculating the square footage of those shapes individually.

## Fact

Local laws dictate whether buyer's agents are responsible for verifying the accuracy of square footage. Most are not. If your buyers have doubts about the square footage estimates stated by the seller or listing agent, ask to see how figures were calculated. If your buyer wants to measure the house, offer guidance but allow the buyer to measure it herself.

### Check Your Drawing

Take a close look at your drawing before you leave the house. Have you clearly marked all interior unfinished space? Should the drawing be more detailed? Are you missing important dimensions? Make the drawing as thorough as possible so that you won't have to return for another measuring session.

If measuring a house seems like too daunting a task, you may want to consider hiring an appraiser, architect, or other qualified professional to measure it for you. Find out what is acceptable in your area. There are times when it is impossible to measure from the outside—snow cover or the slope of the land may make it necessary to measure the property from the inside only. Find out the rules in your area and be sure to follow them exactly.

A successful listing presentation will result in a property for you to market and sell. If you are marketing a property, you have the chance of getting calls on that property, selling that property or another property, and the cycle of success can begin!

Chapter 10

# Marketing Your Listings Locally

**Discovering the best** avenues for marketing your listings locally can be a challenge. There are numerous publications and other media who want your advertising dollars. The promise of capturing the perfect buyer for the house you are advertising can entice you to utilize every method that comes your way.

## *What Are Buyers Looking For?*

It's wonderful to acquire the perfect listing, one that buyers will flock to the minute the for sale sign goes in the yard. But perfect listings can be elusive, so a good listing agent must carefully analyze each property to uncover the features that buyers are seeking. There's something unique and desirable about every listing you'll sign a contract to market. It's up to you to find out what the property has to offer a potential buyer.

Once you've worked in real estate for a while, you will understand what buyers are looking for and instinctively know which features to promote most vigorously in your advertising copy. New agents don't have experience to draw from, so they must do a little detective work to determine which features are most popular in their towns.

The first place to look is in ads written by seasoned agents. Those are the people who usually know what to say to attract buyers. Which features do they mention most prominently? The list will differ for every area but you can bet that if an amenity is mentioned frequently and by many agents, it's something that local buyers find desirable.

Search the sold listings in your MLS, paying close attention to the number of days the properties were on the market before selling. You'll find out right away which neighborhoods are most popular. You might also see a trend in the types of properties that are selling best. Are they two-story homes, single-story ranches, homes with split-bedroom plans, houses with basements, or perhaps houses with large yards? Pay attention to land sales too, and try to determine what makes land attractive to buyers in your area.

### Fact

Your Chamber of Commerce can probably tell you what type of buyers are most plentiful in your area—first timers, senior citizens, young professional couples. Fair Housing guidelines prevent you from mentioning specific demographic groups in your ads, but you can and should mention the features that are attractive to people in those groups.

Analyze your listings to determine which amenities to mention most prominently in your ads. Query your sellers to find out if popular features might be hidden. Are there wood floors under the carpets? Would a little tree-trimming open up a view? Have the sellers made desirable updates that aren't immediately visible, such as plumbing and wiring upgrades? What did they like best about the house when they purchased it?

Your ad-writing tasks will be much easier—and more productive—once you know which features are most popular and how that popularity ties in with your listings.

## *Local Advertising Possibilities*

In addition to promoting local knowledge of your availability as a qualified agent, local advertising offers many options when you are trying to spread the word about one of your listings. Most real estate firms advertise all of their listed properties in specific for-sale publications. Ads for your listings might be included at no cost to you or you might be required to pay for all or a portion of the cost; that's something you discovered in your agent interview. Many agents go beyond the ads provided by their firms, promoting their listings in other ways.

Good old classified advertising is sometimes the best place to advertise your properties. The most optimal days to advertise will vary from town to town, but read the classifieds for a few weeks and you will be able to easily determine which days are best. Your local paper might also publish a regular real estate brochure or section. These special sections of the newspaper devoted to real estate listings are popular with the exact people to whom you are trying to market your listing—buyers who are searching for property.

Other places to consider advertising include:

- Your local cable television channel's information page
- Big-screen ads at a local movie theater
- Ads in neighborhood newspapers
- A page of your own in the publications where your firm advertises
- Glossy home magazines such as *Homes and Land* or the *Real Estate Guide*
- The Internet

One of the most important things you can do to promote your listings is to use directional signs that attract the attention of buyers, starting them at a major street intersection and continuing on to your listed property. Place your larger for sale sign on the property so that it is clearly visible from the street. Be sure to check for the sign ordinances in your area. Some areas only allow one sign at the property and some areas limit the size of the sign.

## Essential

Always ask for an owner's permission before placing a directional sign on private property. In addition to being courteous, you may generate new contacts. You'd be surprised how many people will ask you about the property you are attempting to lead buyers to and sometimes you meet people who are thinking about selling their home.

Buyers are more likely to jot down and remember your name if you purchase special signs, called riders, to attach to the larger sign. Rider signs typically include an agent's name and telephone number.

There are also promotional signs such as Talking House, which is a sign that gives people a brief description of the house when they tune their radio dial to a certain frequency while parked in front. Although these gimmicks are fun, they may not work in your area, so do a little research before investing in them.

## *Getting the Word Out to Other Agents*

We all love to sell our own listings because it increases our earnings and gives us the satisfaction of a job well done. But how many serious buyers do you expect to work with at one time—ten, fifteen, twenty? Chances are that only a few of the buyers you help at any given time are looking for a house with features that match those of your listings.

However, if you multiply each agent who is familiar with your listing by those same numbers, you can see that your pool of buyers increases greatly when other agents show your listings. It's up to you to make sure they have all the information they need to keep your properties on their list of "must shows."

### Postcards and Flyers

Mailing color postcards and flyers to individual agents is one way to get the word out about your listings. You can print them easily yourself, if you have a computer and color printer. You'll need a digital camera (or a traditional camera and scanner) to get the photos onto the computer's hard drive.

If printing and postage is too much of an expense, an alternative is to e-mail a description and color photos to agents in your area. It's best to pick up the phone and call agents to make sure they are receptive to information received via e-mail. The abundance of spam and virus attachments that are floating around cyberspace has made some people reluctant to add more e-mail addresses to their in-boxes.

## E-Alert

Take a day to hand-deliver your flyers or postcards. It's a great way to introduce yourself to area agents. They'll remember you—and your listing—more vividly than they would if you dropped materials in the mail.

Your MLS system probably includes an option to e-mail someone a clickable text link that will open up a page of information about the listing. That might be a good alternative for agents who do not want to receive attachments.

### Local Real Estate Agent Events

Attend local events organized by your MLS or Board of Realtors®. Most offices have regular luncheon meetings and other get-togethers for their agents. Volunteer for a job in the local organization. You aren't qualified to be an officer yet, but there are always committees that need help. Attend as many functions as you can, and get to know your fellow agents. You'll find that a friendly relationship results in a lot more calls about your listings. Be sure to reciprocate by showing their listings to your potential buyers.

## *Good Photos Are Essential*

Photographs provide an important introduction to a property. They are especially critical now that nearly all real estate listings are displayed on the Internet in some form. A good photo helps you grab the interest of buyers and other real estate agents, slowing them down as they flip through the pages and keeping them focused on your listing long enough to read the details about it.

Now that most MLS systems are online, or at least computer-based, it's more common for an agent to sit down in front of a monitor with a buyer and search for suitable listings. The agent can move through them one by one and allow the buyer to choose the properties that are the most interesting. Properties without photos are often overlooked completely. An agent who has viewed your listing in person will know when a photo is not a good representation of it, but buyers don't have that advantage. A poor photo can be an immediate turnoff to someone seeing the listing for the first time, even if the agent tries to convince her that the house "looks much better in person." If you have the ability to add multiple photos to the MLS, do so. Take pictures of the exterior, the view, the kitchen, living room, and other interesting features. Unless it is an unusually luxurious room, avoid bathroom photos.

## Fact

Some of the best house photos are taken on a cloudy day when there is no bright sunshine to create glare. You won't get nice blue skies and white puffy clouds, so zoom in on the house itself. The deeply saturated colors of the house and its surroundings will make up for the loss of sky.

No one expects you to be a professional photographer, but make an effort to take the best pictures possible. You might need to return to the house for photos after you get the listing, to capture the best view. Choose a time when the sun won't be behind the house, glaring into your lens. That arrangement won't produce a quality photograph, even if your camera can compensate for a backlit situation.

Take some sample shots on your first visit to help you preview the best angles to use for the final versions. Inspect the photos to see if they include views that distract from the property, such as children's toys or other items that are scattered about. Are there cars that should be moved? Cars parked in front of open or closed garage doors block the view of the house and make a property appear cluttered. If necessary, ask the owner to tidy up the exterior before you take final photos.

## *Camera and Lens Choices*

A digital camera is one of the best timesaving tools you can buy, and it's an expense that will eventually save you money because it makes film-developing costs a thing of the past. There might be times when it's necessary to print photos, but they'll be specific photos you choose by previewing images in the camera itself or on a computer screen. The technology allows you to bypass developing a roll of film that might only contain a few good shots.

**Essential**

> Don't worry about buying a digital camera yet if expenses are tight. You'll most likely work with buyers before you work with sellers, so photos might not be an issue right away. You can always use a disposable camera to take pictures for out-of-town buyers who ask you to preview properties for them.

Digital images are stored in the camera in tiny square chunks (called pixels), which sit side by side to form the image. The total number of pixels in an image is often stated as megapixels, which means millions of pixels. Sometimes pixels are expressed by giving the total number of pixels in a photo's height and width, such as 1,800 × 1,200 pixels. Multiply those dimensions together to determine the total number of pixels, 2,160,000 in the example—or 2.16 megapixels.

### How Many Megapixels Do You Need?

The more pixels in an image the smaller they each are, resulting in a less jagged, higher-quality image. Most digital cameras are suitable for use in e-mails and online, where lower pixel counts (referred to as *lower resolution*) are the norm. However, your printed images will look better if you choose a camera that produces photos with more pixels (higher resolution).

- 4" × 6" is the maximum print size for a quality 1+ megapixel image

- 8" × 10" is the maximum print size for a quality 2+ megapixel image
- 11" × 17" is the maximum print size for a quality 3+ megapixel image

A 2+ megapixel image is all most real estate agents require, but camera prices have dipped in recent years, so you may want to consider a higher-resolution camera. Most digital cameras have settings that allow you to choose your pixel quality, from low to high. If you choose a lower pixel setting on one of these cameras, you can fit a larger number of pictures on the camera's memory card.

### Lenses and Flashes

Most digital cameras come with a lens that goes from wide angle to zoom. The flexibility helps you frame your shots as you take them, and that means you won't spend as much time cropping unnecessary areas from the photos after they are loaded into your computer.

A single, wide-angle lens is useful, especially for photographing interiors. It allows you to capture a wider area of the image from a closer position. A wide-angle lens will also help you capture the entire house in one image, without walking across the street.

Another thing to consider when shopping for a digital camera is the camera's flash capability. Although nearly all digital cameras have a built-in flash, it's not always powerful enough for indoor photographs. Buy a camera with a hot-shoe, a place where you can plug in a more powerful flash accessory, if you plan to take lots of indoor pictures.

### Storing Your Digital Photos

Your digital images are initially stored on a memory card. Some cards resemble tiny floppy disks and others are cylindrical in shape. Most memory cards that come with cameras do not hold very many photos, especially at high resolutions, so be sure to buy one or more extra cards that do have plenty of memory. Prices for memory cards have come down drastically in recent years, so even those with large storage capacity are affordable.

Once you've taken your photos, you will use a cable or a special card reader to transfer them to your computer. Once they are stored on your computer, you can delete the images from the memory card and use it again to store new pictures.

The camera should come with some type of transfer apparatus and the software required to manipulate your photos once they are stored in a computer, allowing you to crop and enlarge photos to best showcase the property.

## Fair Housing Laws and Your Ads

It's easy to get enthusiastic when you have a great property to describe. You want the ad to be as tempting as possible so that potential buyers will call and ask to go see it—now! It's important to sound excited about a listing's features. It's just as important to make sure your statements comply with federal Fair Housing laws, which were developed to protect the rights of all people who wish to rent or buy real estate.

### E Alert

Some developments have passed state and federal guidelines that allow them to exist as housing for senior citizens. Your ads may state the requirements for residents living in those communities.

Appropriate advertising is simple if you remember two essential rules when you write advertising copy:

- Describe the property, not the type of people for whom you feel it is suitable.
- Never use words that refer to race, color, national origin, religious preference, gender, familial status, or handicaps.

For example, following are inappropriate descriptions for real estate properties:

- Two-bedroom, two-bath contemporary home is perfect for a mature couple
- The kids will feel right at home in this three-bedroom family home
- Home in quiet neighborhood is perfect for elderly Christian lady

Do the problems in the first two ads jump out at you? The words *mature couple*, *kids*, and *family* don't describe the homes; they describe the type of people you think should live in them. The third ad infers that only people of a certain sex or religious preference are welcome.

**Essential**

Pay attention when federal and state Fair Housing laws are discussed in your prelicensing class. If you are found guilty of Fair Housing violations, you can be fined and you can lose your real estate license. Keep up to date on all amendments and additions to the often-changing federal and state Fair Housing laws.

Labeling your properties in a way that suggests that a house would be appropriate only for certain types of people not only violates Fair Housing laws, it discourages consumers in groups that aren't named from picking up the phone and calling you for more information. Describe a property's features, but leave decisions about its suitability to potential buyers.

## Proof Your Ads for Accuracy

Fair Housing isn't the only sensitive issue you must be aware of when writing ads; your ad copy must be accurate. It's easy for misleading words to slip in if you aren't careful. Those words can lead to complaints to your licensing board and even lawsuits after the sale if unhappy buyers feel you misled them about a property's components. To avoid this unfortunate event, make sure you examine each ad carefully to make sure it is accurate.

Following is an example of an ad to examine for accuracy.

> This large contemporary home has been completely updated. It features vaulted ceilings with skylights, a heated sunroom, and a large master bath with a Jacuzzi tub. Another bonus is the hardwood floors that you'll find beneath the carpeting.

The words *completely updated* might indicate a different level of work to different people. Does the phrase refer to cosmetic updates or has the house been renovated more thoroughly, with new plumbing, wiring, heating, cooling, and other systems? It might be better to replace the phrase with *tastefully remodeled* or another more generic term.

Is the bathroom tub really a Jacuzzi fixture? If you're not sure, call it a jetted tub instead. Other commonly misused brand names are Jenn-Air, Whirlpool, and Pergo. Never use a brand name to describe an item unless you are sure of its origins.

Are you positive there are hardwood floors under the carpeting? Have you seen them or has the seller simply told you they are there? Never advertise a feature you haven't seen for yourself.

When you place an advertisement, your reputation and your career are on the line. Be sure to proof every ad for accuracy before it goes to press.

### E Alert

Some houses were designed with wood floors surrounding the perimeter of a room, but only extending inward about twelve inches. Past that space you'll find carpeting with plywood or another sub-flooring material. Don't assume that wood flooring covers an entire floor unless you've pulled the carpets far enough back from the wall to take a look.

Successful marketing will get buyers to look at the home you have listed, but it is price and condition that will actually sell the property. Meet with your sellers every few weeks to see how things are progressing. Show them the marketing you have done and do an updated CMA. Let them know the feedback from the showings you have received. If all the showing feedback mentions something about the condition that can be changed, encourage your sellers to change it. It could be as simple as having the kitchen painted or the carpets cleaned. If you discover, through your new CMA, that the price needs to be adjusted, encourage your sellers to make the change. Marketing is your job, but selling a property is a joint effort between you and your seller; work together to be sure you can get the highest price in the shortest amount of time.

Chapter 11

# Working with Your Sellers

**Acquiring a listing** is only the first step in your career as a real estate listing agent. Now, it's time to work closely with your sellers to market and sell the property for as high a price as possible, and in as short a time as possible. You need the cooperation of your sellers to do that—and they need your guidance and expertise. Developing a balanced, give-and-take relationship with your clients brings success to all.

## *It's a House Now, Not a Home*

Selling real estate is as stressful for sellers as it is for homebuyers, especially when the house isn't quite at its best or problems occur that make everyone wonder if a closing will actually take place. Sellers tend to take everything about a sale personally when the real estate they are selling is a home. Low offers and rude comments from other agents and potential buyers can cause hurt feelings, enough so that sellers sometimes don't even want to negotiate with a qualified buyer if they feel the buyer or someone connected with the buyer has insulted them.

You can help eliminate some of the problems that result in wounded pride by helping your sellers depersonalize their feelings about the residence. It's not truly their home now; it is a commodity they intend to market. Treating the sales event as a business transaction from the very first day helps put sellers into a better frame of mind to review offers and assess all events that take place—without putting a personal spin on them.

Warn your sellers now that low offers are common, that buyers like to negotiate, and not to take it as a personal insult against the house. Wouldn't they like to get the best price for a house they are buying? Preparing them for the realities ahead of time lets them know it's a common situation and not something that, if it occurs, is directed at them.

### Alert

When vacant homes are closed up, without heat or air conditioning, the air can get stale and damp smelling. This is an instant buyer turn-off. Sometimes the interior of a house without heat feels even colder than it is outside. Encourage your sellers to leave heat and air conditioning on, to reduce odors and make the house more inviting.

Becoming familiar with legal documents also helps sellers understand they are involved in a business transaction. Give them a blank, sample copy of the offer to purchase that is used in your area so that they'll have time to study it before an offer is made. Review it with them and explain the standard wording. Be sure to give them sample copies of commonly used additions to contracts, usually called *addendums*. The exact steps you take to get sellers to detach from the house will depend on the individuals, because everyone is different. You'll find that you must balance the desire to make them think of the sale as a business transaction with a bit of empathy about their move, especially if they have many years of memories associated with the house.

### Fact

Professional home stagers are specialized decorators who prepare homes for showings. Sometimes they work with an owner's belongings, but they often bring in their own items to create a mood. These items might include lush plants, overstuffed cushions, wall hangings, and even furniture.

## *Getting the House Ready to Sell*

A large majority of sellers get their houses in shape before real estate agents ever see them. They know a house in good condition usually carries a higher price tag than a house that is only so-so. But you'll encounter some sellers who won't do anything until you make suggestions. Be prepared to help them prioritize tasks to get the house in the best possible shape for buyers to view.

Your sellers can get started by first handling some important tasks inside:

- Make the kitchen spotless; clean the oven and other appliances.
- Strive for shiny clean bathrooms, floor to ceiling.
- Make all rooms neat and tidy.
- Remove clutter.
- Remove furniture that crowds a room.
- Eradicate offensive odors.
- Wash all windows and skylights.

That's a start, and some sellers will stop there. Most sellers, however, will take additional steps to get the house ready to show, once they understand that the work improves their chance of selling faster and for a top price.

### It's Time to De-Clutter

We all have way too much *stuff*, so de-cluttering is one of the most helpful things a seller can do before allowing buyers to see the house. They're planning to move, so they'll have to pack up eventually and there are important reasons for doing it now. Removing all random items from shelves, countertops, or closets makes the house appear more spacious.

Sellers should consider removing large pieces of furniture if they make the house appear crowded. If the house is severely cluttered, the seller can rent a storage unit where boxes and other items can be kept until it's time to move.

**Essential**

It's especially important to make the kitchen appear as spacious as possible. Most of us have items sitting on our kitchen countertops that we don't use every day. They take up space and look messy, so encourage sellers to store those items in a cabinet.

### Finishing Interior Touches

Encourage your sellers to expose desirable features. Are there gorgeous hardwood floors hiding under dated carpets? It makes sense to uncover them if it can be done for a reasonable cost. Are heavy drapes keeping natural light from streaming in? Lighten up the interior by removing them and replacing them with inexpensive ready-made bamboo shades or other light-filtering window coverings.

### Curb Appeal

Many homebuyers decide whether or not to look inside a house based on what they see when they view the house from the street. This is curb appeal. Your seller's goal should be to make buyers start to fall in love with the house from the moment they see it. Home sellers will be closer to accomplishing that if they take care of some important exterior tasks:

- Keep the lawn mowed.
- Sweep the driveway and pressure wash it if necessary.
- Evaluate landscaping and add or remove elements.
- Enhance evening appeal with exterior lighting.
- Spruce up the front door with a good cleaning or fresh paint.
- Clean the gutters and wash exterior windows.
- Paint the house if it's peeling or terribly faded.
- Put away all garden implements and other tools.
- Keep the entrance free of ice and snow.

Every property is different. Help your sellers brainstorm to determine exactly which tasks will be most effective at increasing curb appeal.

## Dealing with Land Sales

Preparing land for sale isn't quite like getting a house ready for potential buyers, but there are some tasks you and your seller must complete before anyone attempts to show it. You must determine the boundaries of the land, mark them, and have a full stock of clear and informative handouts to provide to potential buyers.

**E Alert**

> Vacant land is often shown on a moment's notice. Because there is not an occupied house involved, agents do not often call to make an appointment unless they aren't sure how to find property boundaries. Make it easy for them. Buy outdoor brochure boxes for your land listings and be sure they always contain copies of your handouts.

The first thing you should do is locate the property lines, using brightly colored surveyor's tape to flag permanent markers and any other spots along the boundaries that will help identify the property. The seller should go with you to mark the lines if possible.

A copy of a boundary survey will be a big help to you when you try to locate property lines. If your sellers don't have a survey, they will have to decide whether or not to order one. Visit your county courthouse and ask staff to show you how to determine if a survey for the property was ever recorded. You'll find that owners do not often have copies of older documents.

Prepare handouts for other agents and potential buyers and offer as much information as you can to help them locate property boundaries. The packet could include tax maps, which are available at your county courthouse, surveys, topographic maps, aerial shots, or even a text description that points out identifying features.

## Question

**Does my seller have to pay for a survey for the buyer?**

Customs regarding surveys differ across the United States. In some areas, lenders require surveys to approve a buyer's loan, but sellers are expected to pay for them. In other areas, surveys aren't as critical. Ask your broker-in-charge to tell you how surveys are handled where you work.

Small lots are easier to mark and identify than larger land tracts, but do your best to find property boundaries no matter how large or small the acreage is. You might be surprised how many agents stick a sign on a piece of land but don't bother to determine anything beyond whether the sign is actually on the property. Do those tracts get shown? Not usually. Making a piece of land easy to find is your best ticket to getting it sold.

## *Preparing Home Sellers for Showings*

Successful showings are the result of good preparation by both you and your sellers. You'll find that buyers are more plentiful if you make sure your listings have a reputation among other agents as being homes that are easy to show. You'll need seller cooperation to make that happen, so put yourself on the pathway to sales by explaining some of the intricacies of showings to your sellers.

Most sellers want the house to be in "perfect" condition before a buyer sees it. Sometimes they ask you to put a note on the MLS that a twenty-four-hour notice is required for a showing. What they don't understand is that same-day and last-minute requests are common. They might miss out on a good number of showings by being inflexible. Agents might even stop asking for showings if the sellers deny access too often. Explain that fewer showings equal fewer potential buyers, which increases the time it takes to sell and decreases the demand for the house.

Encourage sellers to keep the house in good showing condition, even if it's not perfect. Buyers can see past a little clutter as long as the house isn't dirty. The easiest way to maintain the house during the time it's on the market is to get the prep work handled before it goes on the market; organize rooms and perform de-cluttering tasks so that ongoing care will be easy.

**Essential**

Showings for tenant-occupied houses must be handled according to your state laws. Learn how much notification you are required to give renters before entering the house. Most states allow access with twenty-four hours advanced notice. Sometimes you can work out special deals with the tenants to shorten that timeframe.

### Keeping It Flexible

Real estate agents try to arrive with their buyers at the scheduled showing time, but sometimes there are delays. Buyers might arrive late for their appointment. They could all be stuck in traffic. Late arrivals are often caused when buyers take longer than planned to look at one or more houses before they get to yours. Hopefully, your sellers are away from the house in anticipation of the showing. Encourage them to stay away a little longer than they think is necessary, so that they don't interrupt the showing when they return.

### Sellers Who Want to Show

Sellers worry that agents and buyers won't be able to view the house adequately unless they are there to show them the fine points. In fact, many want to be present because they are curious about potential buyers and they want to witness buyer reaction to the home.

Make your sellers aware that buyers feel very uncomfortable when a seller is present. They often won't even open closet doors or look into all of the rooms because they fear being rude. It isn't unusual for buyers to try to get away from the house quickly if they feel the seller is watching them. That's not a good scenario for a sale.

### E Alert

Convey showing facts to sellers in a "did you know" tone, rather than telling them what they must and must not do. They are more likely to comply with your requests when they understand that certain actions will help them sell the house and others can slow down the sale tremendously.

Sellers like to talk to buyers, and not just about the house. Buyers might be turned off by the mood of the seller or by a statement the seller makes, causing an early exit. They are there to see the house, not get to know the seller and chitchat about hobbies or the weather—or worse, politics and other controversial topics. It's best for business to keep them apart.

If your seller absolutely will not leave, make sure they understand that it might reduce their chances of a sale. Counsel them to go outside or stay in one location while buyers are there, and not to hover over the buyers and their agent.

## Sellers Who Want You to Be Present

Sellers may not realize when asking you to be present at showings that your presence is an immediate turnoff to other agents. They don't have time to work around your schedule and as previously noted, real estate is a competitive business. Some agents are afraid you'll try to take away or influence their buyers. If the other agent is working as a buyer's agent, she won't feel comfortable discussing the house with her clients if you are there. Explain to sellers that having you around can be the kiss of death to showings and refuse to do it unless there is a very good reason why you should be there.

## Essential

Show that you respect your seller's opinion by asking him what he thinks the home's best features are. Promote those features and others in a flyer, and make sure the seller has a supply of them to leave out for buyers at showings.

Some sellers might ask you to be present if they are worried about the theft of small items from the home. There is no guarantee that you or another agent will see every move a buyer makes, so those items should be packed away before showings begin. Packing them up reduces the chance of theft and keeps buyers from spending their time inspecting an interesting collection instead of looking at the house.

### Controlling Pets

As some people are afraid of dogs and other pets, it's best if they are taken away from the house during showings. If that's not possible, owners should put pets in crates or kennels while buyers are in the house.

While it can be difficult to communicate to sellers that they must follow your guidelines and de-clutter the home, go elsewhere during showings, and put their beloved pets in a kennel for the duration of a showing, try to remember that sellers often simply want to help you get the house sold. Try to figure out a way to give them a role in the sales process, but make sure it's one that is truly helpful and that won't have a negative impact on showings.

## *Helping Your Sellers Make It to Closing*

Successful participation in real estate negotiations is dependent on your complete understanding of local laws and the specific contents of every contract with which you are involved. You'll learn the fine points of deciphering a contract at prelicensing school. Once you're licensed, you'll hopefully get related training from a member of your real estate firm. Although technical negotiations are critical, it is every bit as important to support your clients emotionally and help make sure their path to closing is a smooth one.

One of the most stressful events of the transaction for both sellers and buyers is the home inspection. It's not unusual for everyone to be on edge until they hear the results, even if they think the house will breeze through with no problems. Try to get your sellers to relax. Let them know that if repair issues do occur, they can nearly always be handled so that all parties are happy with the outcome.

If there are serious problems with the house, they should certainly be disclosed to buyers before an offer is made. However, there are several things that buyers *perceive* as problems that truly aren't. Your sellers can keep the home from failing inspection by taking care of a few issues that always make buyers wonder if repairs are needed.

Be sure to remove all traces of mold and mildew inside and outside the house. Remove the source of dampness that allowed them to grow. Cover bare earth in crawl spaces and unfinished basements to place a barrier between the house and the earth. Exposed dirt is a source of moisture that can encourage insects and mold growth.

### E Alert

If buyers ask for repairs, you'll be responsible for helping your seller decide whether or not to make requested changes. Remember that the contract between the buyer and seller plays a crucial role in all repair issues and determines which items can and cannot be included in requests.

Water entering a basement often does so because of poor drainage, not because the foundation needs to be repaired. (Although, the foundation can become an issue over time if the poor drainage is not dealt with properly.) To improve drainage, clean the home's gutters and make sure downspouts are pointed away from the home's foundation, and that in-ground drainage avenues are clog free.

Another way to eliminate potential sources of moisture is to make sure that flashing around the base of chimneys is watertight and that the chimney's mortar and bricks are in good condition. Replace deteriorated shingles if possible.

Your sellers live in the house, so they are probably aware of little things that should be fixed. Make them aware that buyers nearly always question a home's overall condition when their inspection report contains a long list of items that need to be repaired. Handling a long list of little things early on will help them breeze through the inspection later.

## Tracking the Timeline

Your seller's contract outlines many events that must take place before closing. Make a written timeline of those events and keep track of their progress.

- Remind your sellers of tasks they must handle, such as finding a closing agent and preparing documents for that agent.
- If another agent is working with the buyers, call her for required documents, such as loan approval statements and repair requests.

You should also remind your sellers to take care of simple tasks, such as orders to turn off utilities, mail forwarding, and cancellation of insurance on the day of closing. If you're also working with them to buy a house, you might be doing double duty with the tasks at hand to ensure that the purchasing process is running smoothly.

The number one complaint that sellers have about their agent is that they never heard from them. Keeping in touch with your sellers during the listing period and during the escrow period, even if you have nothing new to tell them, will give them comfort and show them you are taking care of their needs.

You'll find that keeping up with the transaction daily helps you tackle problems as soon as they occur. This attention makes problems less stressful for buyers and sellers, and increases the likelihood that they will be resolved. Hang in there and it won't be long before you're sitting at the closing table with your sellers, as they turn over the keys to the property's new owner.

Chapter 12

# Working with Your Buyers

**One thing that** makes real estate so interesting is the diversity of people with whom the agents work. Learning how to deal with different kinds of people is what ultimately trains you to be a good agent. To get started, you simply need a bit of advice about your responsibilities toward buyers and suggestions to help you tune in to their needs. You can take it from there—and have some fun while you're at it!

## *Buyer Clients vs. Customers*

Your state real estate laws dictate the types of working relationships you are allowed to have with buyers and they probably give you the option of working with them as clients or as customers. A buyer client is someone you sign a contract with, agreeing to do everything possible to help her secure the best price on a property and get it to closing. A customer is someone you work with more informally, facilitating the transaction, but without a contract and without as much personal involvement. You must work ethically with both types of buyers but you can offer more in-depth advice to clients than to customers.

Most real estate agents are required to make a written or verbal disclosure during their first contact with buyers, providing them with facts about whom they legally represent. Disclosure usually reveals that the agent works for the property seller, even if the listing is held by another agency. That happens most often when real estate firms belong to an MLS.

An important clarification to know is that a seller's agent is legally bound to work in the best interests of that seller, passing on any information about the buyers that might help the seller obtain a better offer for the property. Buyers working with a seller's agent are customers, and although you must treat them honestly and fairly, you cannot provide them with personal information that violates your contract with the seller, including the seller's bottom dollar or motivations to sell.

Your state laws probably give you the ability to sign a contract with buyers to represent their interests, making you a buyer's agent and turning them into clients. Buyer's agents can advise their clients about nearly any aspect of the transaction, including personal information about the seller, such as an impending divorce or relocation—details that give insights into a seller's motivations to sell.

### E Alert

During disclosure, you must make buyers understand that they should not tell a seller's agent anything they do not want to be repeated to the seller. Making your legal responsibilities clear from the beginning helps you avoid complaints from buyers who are unhappy that their statements are passed on to a property owner.

Many states determine who you are representing by your actions, regardless of how you are being paid. If you are acting as a buyer's agent, even if you do not have a contract with that buyer and even if you are being paid through the MLS by the seller, you may be considered a buyer's agent in the eyes of your real estate commission.

Your role can change if you are a buyer's agent and your buyers decide they want to look at a home listed with your firm. When that happens, you might become a dual agent, as you and your firm are personally contracted with both the buyer and the seller. Dual agency is not allowed in all states and when it is, state law usually requires written acceptance from both the buying and selling clients. Dual agency is a little tricky sometimes, because you must make sure that you protect the confidentiality and needs of both clients.

Some states allow agents to work as facilitators, people who bring the parties together and help them get to closing but who remain neutral and are not advocates for either side. Learn your state laws regarding agent duties and be sure to follow them exactly.

## Fact

While seller's agents cannot disclose personal information about their seller clients, they are obligated to inform buyers of known problems and defects associated with a property, often referred to as *material facts*.

## *Who's Buying and Where Will You Find Them?*

Every real estate market is different. Your buyer pool might consist mostly of young families with children or it could be that the majority of people you'll work with are retirees looking for homes with few steps to climb. You might find that while houses in certain neighborhoods and price ranges are most sought after, your buyers represent a wide range of ages and lifestyles. Once you have an idea who your buyers are, it's easier to find them.

### Searching the MLS

Your local MLS is a good place to begin gathering information about the most popular types of housing in your area. Every MLS system is different but they all have search capabilities that allow you to compile a database of sold properties. The final data entered for each listing includes its sales price, the date sold, the type of financing that was used, and who sold it. However, you're also looking for another ending statistic—its number of days on the market. You can gain valuable information about the market and real estate trends in your area by asking the following questions when exploring your local MLS.

- Which properties sold most quickly?
- Are properties in certain neighborhoods nearly always a quick sale or does a fast turnover have more to do with features?
- What are those features?
- Do you see a popularity trend and if so, does it give you a clue about typical buyers?

It's up to you to decipher the statistics you find and determine how to use them. For instance, a large demand for houses in lower price ranges might mean that your area is good for first-time homebuyers. Look at the financing statistics on sold properties. Are they detailed enough to tell you if buyers acquired FHA loans? FHA loans are a popular mortgage solution for brand-new buyers. If a great number of them are cash sales, you might be dealing with retirees instead of first timers.

## Essential

Visit your local Chamber of Commerce and ask for area demographics, statistics about many aspects of your town, including real estate sales; the printed materials are very helpful. However, they should not take the place of your own research, which gives you a more personal understanding of pricing vs. features—knowledge that helps you work effectively with buyers *and* sellers.

Take a drive to some of the popular neighborhoods you discovered through your research. What types of people live there? Do you see a lot of children playing in yards? Does it appear to be mostly senior citizens? Perhaps it's a neighborhood filled with young professional couples. It's just as possible that you'll see a wide variety of age ranges in the community. Browsing neighborhoods is a great way to become accustomed to your area and helps you answer questions from potential buyers.

### Put the Statistics to Work

Once you've determined that your area is filled with first-time buyers, go find them. How about holding a "how to buy a home" seminar at a local community center? Mortgage brokers, home inspectors, surveyors, and other professionals involved with the home-buying process would very likely help you, because the event would promote their businesses too.

Insert a regular classified ad in your local newspaper's "homes for sale" category. Promote yourself as an agent who can help first-time homebuyers. Talk to lenders first, to make sure you indeed know what it takes to help first timers buy a home.

Visit your post office to learn how to send a bulk mailing to all residents of large apartment complexes. People who rent are always potential buyers. Talk with property managers to find out if the complex has a newsletter and if it accepts ads. If the complex is managed by a real estate firm, they probably won't offer you much help, but if they are not managed by a real estate firm, you have a great chance of getting an ad in their newsletter and of being the agent they refer tenants to.

The type of action you must take depends on the types of buyers you want to target. Brainstorm with other agents in your office to come up with a plan to find them.

## *Building Rapport with Buyers*

You'll have a more successful and satisfying career if you learn how to build rapport with your buyers. They aren't a statistic; they are real human beings who depend on you to help them find what they're looking for and to follow through on the steps to help them obtain it.

We sometimes tend to be more clinical when we talk to buyers on the phone, asking them questions to help us determine what they want and need. But when we meet them face to face, it's important to build rapport by being more personal. Make your buyers feel comfortable about you and the surroundings. How was their trip to the office? Would they like something to drink, or a snack? Point out the restrooms and ask them if there's anything they need before you sit down to consider properties.

Rapport-building discussions help you become familiar with their needs, especially if they're looking for a home:

- Do they have children? How old are they? Do they like their school? Do they want to stay in the same school district?
- What are their hobbies? Do they devote a certain part of their living space to hobby areas?

- Do they prefer to live a short distance from work, or is a lengthier drive okay?
- Do they like to entertain?
- Why did they decide to move?

Each question you ask will lead to other questions. Some questions will help you get to know them as people, and others will help you determine what type of property they desire.

## Fair Housing for Buyers and Renters

Fair Housing comes into play when you show rental or for-sale real estate to consumers. You won't put yourself at risk if you use the same basic guidelines you use for ads (explained in Chapter 10) and make them apply to your showings. In other words, don't show properties based on your personal opinions of where people should live. Leave the decisions to them. During your work as an agent, you cannot take discriminatory action against buyers and renters based on race, color, national origins, religion, gender, familial status, or handicaps. Those actions include:

- Refusal to rent or sell housing
- Refusal to negotiate for housing
- Making housing unavailable
- The decision to deny a dwelling based on the protected classes
- Setting different terms, conditions, or privileges for different people interested in the sale or rental of a dwelling
- Providing different housing services or facilities for different people
- Falsely denying that housing is available
- Denying access to or membership in a facility or service that's related to the sale or rental of housing (such as the MLS)
- Persuading owners, for a profit, to sell or rent by convincing them that the racial makeup of a neighborhood will soon change in a negative way, a tactic known as blockbusting

New agents sometimes confuse the terms *steering* and *blockbusting*. Steering occurs when real estate agents purposely direct consumers to or away from a specific neighborhood to keep the neighborhood's current makeup intact. Though steering usually involves racial issues, it is illegal for any reason. While you cannot steer your buyers to or away from specific neighborhoods, a buyer can tell you he does or does not want to view properties in specific areas. Leave the choices to your buyers.

## Separating Buyers from Browsers

It's important to find out early on if your buyer prospects are serious about buying now. Can they buy if you find the right property today or must they sell another property first? Most people won't give you that information until you ask for it and the answer might save you a lot of time.

### Essential

Offer to visit curious buyers at home so that you can create a comparable market analysis (an opinion of the market value of their property). They probably won't know what they can afford for a new home until they know their property's worth. Offer your services and you might have a new listing as well as a new buyer client.

Buyers who must sell a house before they buy shouldn't spend a great deal of time looking at properties unless their house is already on the market. Give them MLS sheets and talk to them about what's available, but don't spend days showing them houses until you know they are serious about buying.

## Getting Buyers Preapproved for a Loan

Buyers should always be preapproved for a loan before they look at real estate. There are so many loan products available that most people have no way of truly knowing what they can spend until they talk with a mortgage professional. Until they know their limits, it will be difficult for you to search for homes that suit their needs.

If you are working with buyers as clients, ask them to give the mortgage person permission to discuss their file with you. Seller's agents don't usually have as much information about the finances of their customers but it is appropriate to ask for written verification that they qualify for a loan in the general amount of the properties you are showing them.

### E Alert

If your clients are reluctant to get preapproved, remind them that a preapproval letter submitted with an offer shows a seller they are qualified to buy. The letter is a powerful addition to any offer to purchase.

In some locations, real estate agents regularly "qualify" buyers to help determine how much they can afford to spend on a new house. That information might be helpful but it really doesn't tell you much, as the estimate won't be made using an in-depth credit history. Send buyers to a lender for preapproval if you want a true picture of their ability to purchase real estate.

In higher end markets, many of the buyers are savvy and have purchased several homes over the past few years. In these markets, the buyers know they are qualified and will be insulted if you ask them to get preapproved with a lender. Many of these buyers may actually pay cash. Check with your broker or another agent in your office to see what is customary in your marketplace when dealing with higher priced properties.

## Determining Their Wants and Needs

Most buyers come to you with a preset notion of the features their new property must have. You'll find that their wants lists often include a group of amenities that are not available in a single property. When the perfect property is nowhere to be found, it's up to you to help buyers analyze their wants and needs to determine which features are the most important.

Buyers often start adjusting their wants and needs list when you start showing them properties. They discover, on their own, that a specific combination of features is nearly always elusive, even when price is not an issue. When price is an issue, finding everything they are looking for becomes even more difficult.

You'll be surprised how many buyers have a complete reversal of their wants and needs lists as they start viewing properties. They find that some things just aren't feasible, and sometimes they see and like features they didn't even think about.

So how do you know what they really want? Pay attention and ask a lot of questions, avoiding questions that can be answered with a "yes" or a "no." Don't ask them if they want a large kitchen; instead, ask them how they'll use their kitchen. Buyers who love to cook and entertain won't be happy with the tiny galley kitchen that people who dine out might prefer.

## Know Your Inventory

You'll waste a lot of time showing buyers unsuitable properties if you aren't familiar with what's for sale in your area. MLS sheets give you the facts and a few photos but that's not a substitute for a firsthand look at real estate.

If your MLS holds open houses for listings, attend them. If open houses are not an option, ask to preview properties on your own. Some agents at other firms might be more open to previews if several agents attend, especially if a property is occupied and the owner must leave. Vacant properties are easier, because you won't disturb anyone by doing a preview. Make it a point to drive by at least three listings a day. You'll be surprised how many of them appear very different than they do on the MLS.

Buyers are more comfortable working with an agent who they feel has a good grasp on area properties. You'll find that it is much easier to match buyers with properties when you have a firsthand opinion of listings.

### Take Charge of the Showings

Don't become one of those agents who sits by the computer with buyers, allowing them to dictate what they see based on an MLS sheet. It doesn't work. Buyers often eliminate a property because they don't like the photograph, which is always a bad idea. Real estate agents are not professional photographers. Listings can't be judged by a photo or by a three-sentence description.

**E Alert**

> Even though you should avoid allowing clients to control your time (it's as valuable as theirs) there will be many occasions when you can only show a home or take a listing appointment in the evening, or when a weekend is the only time you can write up an offer. If you're committed to success, you'll do the work.

Do let your buyers browse listing sheets but be prepared to explain that seeing a property in person is the only way to know if it's suitable. Knowing your inventory is a must and so is a continued good rapport with buyers. They'll be more receptive to your suggestions when they know you are sincere about helping them.

## Personal Safety Concerns

Although you would like to feel confident about the character and good intentions of your buyer, as a real estate agent you should always be cautious when showing property and aware of potential dangers that you may encounter. Because of the very nature of showing property, you are often in a somewhat secluded place (an empty home) and are alone with individuals you do not know well.

The number of real estate agents who have been robbed, raped, and killed while showing property has grown in recent years. These dangers have forced agents who have traditionally felt comfortable dealing one-on-one with the public to become more cautious. Many offices have responded by developing a series of safety procedures to help protect its agents from harm. Even if your office does not have safety procedures in place, you can minimize your risk of attack by staying alert and following a few basic guidelines.

It's essential to have some type of verifiable information about prospects before showing properties. If you can reach them by calling a home phone number or a work number, chances are the person is not trying to be evasive about his identity. Try to get as much information about him as possible including his e-mail address, home address, cell phone number, and other identifying facts.

### Fact

An agent attending a showing alone could have a partner meet her at the property. Always follow safety procedures, no matter how nonthreatening your prospect might appear.

Never meet customers whom you do not know at a property. Ask them to come to your office, where others will see them, and where someone can note their license plate number and the type of vehicle they are driving. Some real estate firms require a copy of each customer's driver's license before allowing their agents to show properties. Before you leave, give someone in your office an itinerary of the properties you will be showing and have that person call your cell phone occasionally to check on your status.

Do not allow an unknown customer to drive you to properties. You have no control over an abusive situation when you are a passenger in a car. Use your own vehicle for showings or have the customer follow you in her vehicle. If you are threatened as you drive, and instructed to change routes, don't do it! It is much easier to get away from someone in a public place than in the isolated locations where most criminals take their victims.

## E Alert

If you are threatened by a passenger as you drive, hit the brakes to startle your attacker. If you're on a city street, pull the passenger side door so close to another vehicle that it can't be opened, then open your door and run, making as much noise as you can to get attention.

Below are other important safety tactics.

- Keep your cell phone in your pocket, with 911 and the office number programmed for speed-dial.
- Devise a code word or phrase that everyone in the office recognizes as a plea for help.
- Carry pepper spray or mace with you at all times.
- Do not work an open house by yourself.
- Pay attention to floor plans—know your exits.
- Do not show properties to unknown prospects after dark.

Trust your instincts. If a situation doesn't feel right, ask your broker-in-charge or another agent to accompany you on the showing. You'll all feel much safer and more confident when you work together to ensure each other's well-being.

## *Dealing with Buyer's Remorse*

All real estate agents encounter cases of buyer's remorse, a phenomenon that affects many homebuyers. It usually begins shortly after the purchase contract has been accepted. Is it really a good house? Did I pay too much? Can I afford it? Is there a better house out there? These are only a few of the questions that haunt buyers. Once you understand why remorse occurs, you will be in a better position to help your buyers avoid it, or to get them over the hurdles if symptoms have already begun.

A home is the largest purchase most people ever make, so it's a given that buyers want to be absolutely sure their choice is a good one. Nearly every homebuyer has some level of doubt about his purchase, but for many buyers it becomes an obsession. They cannot stop analyzing the transaction and worrying about all the negative "what ifs" that *could* take place, no matter how unlikely they are to occur. Although buyers who seem worrisome throughout the home search process are more likely to have problems, buyer's remorse can affect anyone.

### Fact

Some buyer fears are valid, such as those that occur when a home inspector discovers a house is in need of more repairs than they wish to deal with. Look at the problem objectively to determine which fears are unrealistic and which signal that your buyers should indeed think about ways to cancel the contract.

## Family and Friends Create Doubt

Younger buyers often become remorseful after talking with their parents about their purchase. Parents rarely believe that a house is good enough for their children and they nearly always think the kids paid too much. They might not be in tune with market trends or they might resent not being asked for an opinion before the contract was signed.

Friends and other family members can create doubts too, especially if they haven't purchased real estate for a while or if they live in a part of the country where home prices are much lower. It's typical for people who don't understand the market to tell buyers they paid "way too much" for a home when, in fact, the price was close to true market value. Problems begin when buyers begin to believe the comments. It's your job to reassure your buyers about the home's condition and value.

## Agents Are Sometimes to Blame

Many cases of buyer's remorse can be tracked back to a real estate agent who isn't following through on his duties. Some agents think that showing houses and getting a contract are their primary jobs and that, after those events take place, they can sit back and relax until closing. If that's what you think a real estate agent does, it might be best to consider another career. Getting a signed contract only marks the beginning of your responsibilities.

## E Alert

You will meet buyers whose nature it is to be overly cautious and analyze everything. They may come up with unrealistic worries and far-fetched scenarios. Be prepared to answer a never-ending series of questions for the perpetually nervous buyer.

There are many steps you must keep up with, on an almost daily basis, if you expect to get your buyers and sellers to the closing table. The appraisal, loan progress, inspections, and contingencies that can make or break a contract are just a few of the tasks you must closely monitor. Buyers usually aren't savvy about common problems that occur during a home purchase. That is why they need you. When problems do crop up, your job is to step in with a cool head and offer guidance to help resolve them. If you neglect your buyers they'll begin to stress about even small issues and, in no time, you'll be dealing with a case of buyer's remorse.

### Helping Them Through It

The best thing you can do to help your clients overcome buyer's remorse is to show them why they originally felt the house was *the one* for them. You probably have a list of their wants and needs somewhere, or notes you made while working with them, that serve the same purpose. Read your notes and make some observations.

- Does the house under contract fit the description of the house they were looking for?
- What qualities made the buyers choose this house over others you showed them?

- Were there many possible choices, or was this house the only one that was suitable?
- How long did it take to find the house?
- Is it realistic to think that there is another house available that fits as many of their wants and needs?
- What features of this house did the buyers seem to be most excited about?

Making an honest assessment of the events leading up to the contract will help you discuss the transaction with your buyers. Remind buyers of the reasons they chose the house, but never try to force a buyer into a sale. Refer anyone who decides to break a contract to a real estate attorney for advice about the potential legal repercussions of that action.

## *Getting Buyers to the Closing Table*

The progression from contract to closing differs throughout the United States but there's a common set of issues that real estate agents must monitor to ensure that their buyers complete the transactions. Keeping in constant contact with everyone who plays a part in the process helps you guide your buyers to the closing table, with fewer bumps along the way. It also ensures that you hear about problems as soon as they occur, which gives you an opportunity to help solve them before they stall the closing.

If your buyer is getting a loan to pay for the property, talk with the lender immediately. Ask for a list of all items they require for closing, such as an appraisal, a boundary survey, and specific types of tests and inspections. Your buyers might require the services of a real estate attorney or a title insurance office. Find out who is responsible for ordering the services and monitor the progress to make sure tasks are handled.

## Fact

Lenders typically order reports from appraisers they know, but buyers are usually responsible for finding and contracting with surveyors and inspectors. Do not steer clients to a specific service provider, but do provide them with a list of area professionals who can help with the necessary tasks.

The contract probably contains contingency clauses that give your buyer time to evaluate certain aspects of the purchase. Contingencies cover events that must or must not take place, or give buyers the opportunity to examine facts about the property that are not known when the contract is signed. If contingencies are not met, the buyer can walk away from the contract. Typical contingencies include:

- Home inspections to verify a house is in the condition represented by the sellers
- Boundary surveys to verify that property lines are as stated and that no structures have been built on the lines
- A title search to ensure that the property will be free of liens when it closes
- The ability of the buyer to obtain financing

In some areas of the country, you will be involved in the actual work that's done to satisfy contingencies. In other areas, you won't be directly involved but it's up to you to keep track of their progress and to help negotiate solutions if problems are encountered.

Be sure to remind your buyers of important last-minute details. Have they satisfied the lender's proof of insurance requirement? Have they arranged for utility services? Have they made plans to change the locks on all doors?

You have more responsibility to a client than a customer. No matter what your role is, it is your duty to make sure that the transaction proceeds as smoothly as possible to closing. Make sure that paperwork keeps flowing and that all tasks associated with closing progress as they should. These might include:

- Making sure the buyer has submitted all necessary paperwork to a lender
- Checking the status of an appraisal
- Coordinating home inspections, surveys, and other required tasks
- Submitting requests for repairs and negotiating repair agreements
- Monitoring the loan's progress after everything has been submitted to the lender
- Helping your buyer find a closing agent and keeping in touch with that agent
- Reviewing the HUD-1 Settlement Statement with your buyer

Your personal involvement with getting your buyers to closing depends a great deal on your local customs and laws. If you have any doubts about your duties, ask your broker-in-charge for insight into your role.

Chapter 13

# Perfecting Your People Skills

**Salespeople tend to** be so busy talking that they forget to pay attention to what their clients and customers are saying. You'll find that your efforts are much more effective once you understand that your job is not to sell people real estate—it's to find them houses or other properties they love. To do that you must slow down a bit. Listen to what your clients are saying and learn how to interpret their words and actions and to decipher their wants and needs.

## *Start a Dialogue*

You'll encounter all types of buyers and sellers during your real estate career—not just different personalities, but people who enter the market for different reasons. Basic categories of buyers and sellers include growing families who need larger homes, seniors who want to scale down or live in a one-level residence, people who might not want to move at all but are forced to do so by job relocation or a downturn in their available income. You'll work with investors who are buying rental units, people looking for vacation homes, and people who want to buy a piece of land to build on now or hang on to until a later time.

People you work with don't always tell you their motivations for buying and selling real estate. This is not necessarily because they're being evasive, but because they don't understand the steps you must go through to find what they are looking for. It's up to you to interact with clients in a way that uncovers the facts you need to know to do your job.

To succeed in real estate you will also need to be a careful listener. Does your mind ever jump ahead of the conversation? This happens to most people, often because we can't wait to get our point across to the other person. In real estate, it sometimes occurs when an agent thinks he has to get out all of a preformatted spiel about himself or the property he's showing. He's focusing on what he'll say next instead of listening to the person he is with, who might be trying to describe the perfect property for her needs.

### Fact

Remember, unless they are relocating to another area, your sellers can become buyer clients. You can even work with sellers who are moving to another area by finding them a real estate agent at their new location—and asking that agent to pay you a referral fee when the transaction closes.

Pay careful attention to people when they speak to you. If you're nervous or the type of person who forgets details, keep a pen and notebook handy and jot down comments about important aspects of the conversation. Stay alert to even casual statements that might provide insight to a person's wants or needs.

## Asking the Right Questions

It's not unusual for an inexperienced real estate agent to show a buyer a series of properties he thinks matches the buyer's wants and needs perfectly, then end up writing an offer for something entirely different—or not writing an offer at all because the buyer loses interest when the agent can't locate the "right" property.

One reason for the problem is a lack of effective communication between the agent and the customer. Being a good listener and carefully observing your customers' reactions aren't quite enough to help you discover their true desires. To do that you must ask questions that encourage them to talk.

Agents get accustomed to drilling down a standard list of questions because they know that the short answers will easily slip in to search fields in the MLS database. How many bedrooms and baths do you need? Do you want a home with a basement? Do you need a garage or is a carport satisfactory? The short answers give you information but they don't tell you how your client uses a home, and that's what you need to know to find the best property for each individual.

Queries that encourage someone to talk about his or her needs are sometimes called *open-ended* questions. They end in a way that requires a descriptive response instead of a "yes" or a "no," or an answer that repeats a portion of what the agent asks. Consider the differences between these two similar questions:

- Do you prefer a house on a large lot or a small lot?

This question won't generate much discussion. The client's answer will probably be short and to-the-point.

- How do you like to use your outdoor space?

This question encourages conversation. You might discover that your client doesn't like to mow a lawn and prefers to spend most of her time indoors. This would alert you to focus on homes with smaller or low-maintenance lots.

Open-ended questions are just as appropriate for conversations with sellers. You'll get a much more detailed response by asking, "What steps, if any, do you plan to take to get the house ready to show?" instead of, "When will the house be ready to show?" You'll find that open-ended questions lead to comments that trigger more questions from you and more dialogue with your clients. That opens the door for suggestions from you, which center on actions that will help them sell.

Of course, not all of your questions will be open-ended. You'll need some of those short answers to narrow down a search for a buyer or to help clarify the needs of a seller, but do try to perfect your questioning techniques to draw out as much information as you can in order to work effectively as an agent.

## *Understanding Sellers*

Your people skills are especially necessary when you are exploring the wants and needs of the seller. Understanding sellers can be a little harder than understanding buyers. As buyers move through a house, you will see signs of what they like and don't like and will be able to make adjustments in what you show them.

## Essential

When your clients ask a question and you must give them an answer they may not like (such as the fact that their house is worth less than they expect), ask, "May I tell you the truth?" Your openness encourages them to tell you the truth (such as the fact that they are going to be in foreclosure soon).

A seller may have a different agenda—and may or may not tell you what that agenda is. If the seller only wants to sell because he has to, you will find he is less motivated and more difficult to deal with than if he *wants* to sell. If a seller is having financial difficulties, he may be too embarrassed to talk about it.

## Who's In Charge?

When you work with a couple or other partner groups of buyers or sellers, you'll discover that one person often dominates the information-gathering and decision-making process. It's important to treat all of your clients and customers with care, but learning to detect which of your buyers or sellers has the lead role in the transaction helps you convey important details to the right person.

Watching your clients as they interact with each other and with you is sometimes all it takes to determine which person will make the decision to buy or sell. When you ask a question, does one person hesitate or glance at the other to look for an answer instead of responding to you? Does one client seem to be in charge of financial matters?

Those are both common scenarios that can help you determine who is in charge, but the clues are often more subtle, and there's no magic trick to figuring out which one it is other than paying close attention as you work with your clients.

## E Alert

Make eye contact with each person in the transaction. If your clients bring a family member or friend along, make eye contact with that person as well. Eye contact is one way your clients gauge how important you think they are.

Sometimes one person is in charge in public but the other is in charge in private. Do not focus exclusively on the person you consider to be the decision-maker. The other person may not appear in charge but may be the one who decides not to use you if you are not giving her attention as well. Try to keep your attention as even as possible on all parties involved.

### Parental Influences

The opinions of parents can influence the decisions of young singles or couples who are buying their first home. Some parents are unrealistic about the type of home a first timer can buy. This is especially true if they haven't bought or sold real estate for a while, so they tend to be overly critical of nearly every home. Your young clients might be comfortable with a fixer-upper or starter house, but the parents might discourage that because it will be "too risky" or "too much work."

Your best approach is to educate all of your clients about the home-buying process and do your best to find them a house they love. Give them the information they need to discuss with their parents. Try not to get involved in those discussions yourself, especially if you feel they could turn into arguments.

Parents are parents forever and you're a fleeting part of the young buyer's life, but you can indeed offer a helpful and stabilizing presence if you let the buyer know he can count on you for the facts he needs.

## Essential

If your clients seem very young, you should probably ask them to show you identification that verifies they are old enough to enter into a legal real estate contract. Minors can buy property, but contracts signed by minors are not enforceable.

### Other Influences

Some people like to get direction from many different sources. They may depend on their parents for some ideas, but what a friend said or what they read in a newspaper article can have an impact on them as well. If their friend bought in a certain school district or bought a certain style of house, the friend may try to influence your clients as well. Sometimes well-meaning friends will give your clients poor or outdated advice. Work at building your clients' trust in your ability as a professional. Do not discount their other sources, but show them that your points are as valuable, if not more so, due to your expertise in real estate.

## *Are They Telling You Everything?*

You'll discover early on that buyers don't always give you all the facts about their ability to buy real estate. Sellers aren't always honest about the condition of a structure or financial circumstances that make selling a necessity. Both situations give you more practice in developing your people skills and drawing out the information they are reluctant to reveal.

### Buyers' Financial Concerns

Buyers who ask to see owner-financed or lease-to-own properties are sometimes sending you a signal that they don't think they can obtain a mortgage. Some know they have credit problems and others don't think they can handle the down payment and closing costs. It's up to you to help them determine if they really can buy. There are loans out there for people in all types of financial circumstances and there are sellers who will help pay a buyer's closing costs in order to move a property. Letting people know all of the options available will make them more open with you about which option to choose.

Giving too many negative but vague opinions about multiple properties is another clue that buyers aren't ready to buy or don't really think they can purchase a home. When asked what they think about a house or other real estate, these buyers might respond with, "It didn't feel right" or, "We want to think about it." Buyers who are ready to buy don't hesitate to tell you exactly what they didn't like about a property.

Use your best questioning tactics and people skills to uncover the real reasons behind their hesitation. Once you know why someone does not think they can commit to a purchase, you'll be in a better position to show them how they can actually make it happen.

### Sellers with Financial Difficulties

Sellers who are having financial difficulties are not always ready to disclose it to you. Experiencing financial hardship is embarrassing for anyone, and sellers in the midst of dealing with these troubles may be hoping you will sell the house before they have to deal with foreclosure or other court actions, and therefore may not feel it is necessary to inform you of their troubles.

Staff in the public records departments at your local courthouse can show you how to find out if there are liens or debts against the property or if a foreclosure is already in the works. You might also find judgments against properties during your search, liens put into effect by the court system. Many of the more populated counties have placed this information online although it is often not as up to date as the records in the county offices themselves. There are also online services that will do the research for you for a nominal fee. Your local title company may also be willing to do the research for you. They may or may not charge a fee, depending on how much work is involved.

Most people have a mortgage and many people have second mortgages, also known as *home equity loans*. It's good to have information about those loans, but you're mostly looking for judgments and liens filed by roofers, appliance companies, and others because they weren't paid for work done at the house. Too many liens send up a red flag that the owners are having financial difficulties.

### Question

**What is a lien?**

A lien is a legal claim one person has on the property of another person to ensure the payment of a debt. In other words, in the case of a lien, the property is collateral.

Gather this information before you show up for your listing appointment. If you think the sellers are in trouble, manipulate the conversation to talk about the amount they will net from the sale.

Some sellers don't realize that liens must be paid in full at closing unless a lien holder agrees to a reduced payoff (something you can help them do). Mention payoff facts in a casual way without alerting the sellers that you suspect they have problems. Once the conversation heads in that direction most sellers will begin to open up to you, especially if you offer suggestions for getting the house sold and helping them through their problems.

Sometimes telling the seller a story about another individual (imaginary, of course), as if it is not their issue but someone else's, can help ease them into telling you their situation.

## *What Do Buyers Really Want?*

While all buyers have a unique way of determining which house is right, they all want a house that will feel like "home." Even if it is not perfect in other ways, that sense of home makes it easier for buyers to justify the purchase. Buyers are trying to fulfill many different needs with a home purchase. Your clients' needs will vary, and the same need may not be fulfilled in the same way for each client. They can't always put these needs into words, but the underlying requirements are there.

Buyers may insist on granite countertops, without truly realizing it is the prestige they are after. Buyers who say they want "a view" may really be looking for privacy. The underlying need for privacy or prestige might be met by a property without a view or granite countertops, but your client won't know that unless he sees it and feels good about the property.

Granite countertops and a view are specific, stated benefits some buyers look for to satisfy their needs. Determining the needs that underlie those requirements will help you point out the benefits of a home that lacks granite or a view, but may actually satisfy the need. The needs the average buyer wants his new home to fulfill can be summed up in this list:

- **Value:** a quality home for a good price
- **Prestige:** prestigious surroundings; a house to impress others
- **Convenience:** easy access to work, school, stores, etc.
- **Security:** a secure house in a safe neighborhood
- **Comfort:** a comfortable, "warm" home
- **Aesthetics:** an attractive home
- **Privacy:** a private location; privacy-conscious architecture and landscaping
- **Entertainment:** easy access to entertainment; the ability to entertain at home
- **Health:** climate and facilities to promote health and well-being
- **Recreation:** easy access to recreational facilities
- **Education:** an exceptional school district or other educational facilities

This list is based on a list of basic human needs created by psychologist Abraham Maslow, who practiced during the era of Sigmund Freud and B. F. Skinner. His "Hierarchy of Needs" is represented by a pyramid, which shows the progression of human needs. The base of the pyramid represents the most basic needs (food, shelter, and warmth), and as you progress upward to the top of the pyramid, you see the more advanced requirements, such as the need to belong and gain recognition. The previous list is expanded for its relationship to real estate. It addresses the higher human needs, nearer the top of Maslow's pyramid, and assumes the more basic needs have been met.

## Essential

The key to making a home desirable to buyers is to point out features that satisfy the basic needs that are important to that specific buyer. It is important to tailor your highlighted features to match that particular buyer's needs, as some features represent different benefits to different buyers and satisfy different needs.

When you show property, take note of the features the buyer chooses to comment on. Begin to discern the benefits and needs to which they are tied. If they don't volunteer the information, ask them about the homes they have seen. What did they like or dislike about them? What specific features made one home better or not as good as others? Careful listening will help you determine the benefits your buyer seeks to satisfy her needs.

Most buyers will have two or three primary needs that must be satisfied in order to purchase a home and, inevitably, some needs that are more important than others.

If you show a buyer a lot of properties and he makes no offers, consider that you may be missing one of his basic needs. As value is one of the basic needs, be sure you are shopping in the right price range. Pay attention to your client—you may see a trend. Close proximity to schools and shopping may satisfy the "convenience" need. A home with formal furnishings may put off a buyer who is looking for comfort. If you realize that comfort is a hot button for your buyers, you can remind them that the furniture does not stay and the house has a cozy feel were it not for the formal décor.

Here is an example of a buyer whose hidden need was expressed as a requirement: A woman insisted on many safety features, including an alarm system and no sharp edges on counters or hearths. She said she wanted her three small children to be safe at home. Her agent understood her need for safety, and he showed her several one-story houses, assuming they were safer than houses with stairs. She did not like any of them. After the third one-story house, the agent asked her why a one-story house would not work for her. The woman explained that she was worried someone would climb in a bedroom window and take one of her children. So, a two-story house, with the bedrooms upstairs, was a safety feature the woman really wanted.

As a real estate agent, you can discern many clues to what your client sees as the perfect home. No one wants to criticize someone else's home, but if your clients offer vague comments, such as "It's not my style," be sure to interview further. See if you can get more information by asking about their style. Remember to ask open-ended questions. Each little bit of information will help complete the puzzle.

E Alert

Pay attention to the needs that are *most* important to your buyer and try to select properties that fulfill them. You may not find a property that satisfies your buyer's *every* need, but you will find many that come close, which may lead to an offer.

## More Than Listening

Learning body language will also help you better understand the needs of your clients. If the seller crosses his arms when you talk about money, it may be a subject that he is uncomfortable with or you may be telling him something he does not want to hear (such as he needs to reduce his price). If a buyer taps her foot or acts impatient while waiting for her enthusiastic husband to finish viewing a property, it may be a house that they will not be able to agree on. Sometimes the signs are more subtle and you may not pick up on them right away. Be as observant as possible to notice when one of your clients or customers gives an unspoken sign of their approval or disapproval of a property.

With practice you will be able to understand more and more the verbal as well as nonverbal signs that your clients and customers give you.

Chapter 14

# After the Sale

**Real estate transactions** can be a challenging experience for every person involved in getting them to the closing table. You can pat yourself on the back for making it from listing to the closing table successfully! Take a breather from current clients after a closing but not for long, because it's essential for your future business to keep them informed about the services you can provide to them or to their friends.

## *Closing Gifts They'll Appreciate*

Many agents give their clients a closing gift at the end of each successful real estate transaction. You've been through a lot of steps together to get to the closing table, sometimes difficult and stressful events. A gift is an extra way to say, "Thank you for your business."

### Personal Gifts

Try to tailor your gifts to suit each client. A gardener would appreciate a plant or gift certificate from a local nursery. Bird lovers might like a birdhouse to place outside at their new home. Quality wind chimes that play melodic tones are another possibility. Personal gifts have one thing in common: they are items your client will keep and they'll remember you when they look at them. Pay attention to each client's interests as you work with them and you'll find that personal gifts are not usually difficult to choose.

### Helpful Gifts

Your buyer clients might be camping out at their new house for a day or two before their furniture and other belongings are moved. Giving them a gift certificate for a popular local restaurant would be a quick and easy way for them to have a relaxing meal out.

If you have the equipment, take a photo of your buyers' new house and put it into your computer. Use the photo to design and print postcards they can send to friends and family who might not see the house in person for a while. Be sure to include your buyers' new mailing address.

### E Alert

The Internal Revenue Service limits the amount you may deduct for a closing gift for any one transaction. You can certainly spend more if you wish, but be careful to only deduct the amount allowed by law. Check with your state's real estate division as well; the value of some gifts may put them into the "kickback" category and may not be allowed.

Some agents who work for franchised firms have the option of giving their clients a subscription to their parent franchise's homes magazine. All are publications that feature renovation and decorating ideas.

There are an endless number of possibilities for closing gifts. Determining an appropriate and thoughtful closing gift should be fun, and it will not be difficult if you've become acquainted with your clients during the transaction. Start thinking about it long before closing day and you'll be able to come up with a gift your clients will appreciate and remember.

## Community Gifts

If your clients are new to the area, you may want to consider a gift that connects them to the community. If there are history or picture books about the region, this can make a great closing gift. It gives your client a chance to learn about the area and feel more connected to it. You may also want to create your own book of referrals to local businesses. Your clients will appreciate knowing whom to call for gardening services, a haircut, or for home repairs. Ask the local service people and businesses that you recommend to offer your clients a coupon, which you can include in the book.

## Ongoing Contact

You'll see some of your clients more often than others. People who share your hobbies or interests might be in the same clubs or organizations. Your client might be a fellow member in your religious organization. Maybe your client is someone who works in the grocery store where you shop regularly. But even if you see them frequently, will they remember to mention your name to family and friends who want to buy or sell real estate?

### Fact

Buyers new to an area may depend on you to direct them to other services such as a good doctor or car mechanic. Be sure your clients and customers know that you are their agent, even after the sale has gone through.

Most people need to be reminded that you are in the real estate business. Add every client to the database you started when you first became an agent. Flag their names in some way (either manually or in a computer program) to make them stand out as true clients, not simply casual contacts who might be interested in buying or selling.

Using a software spreadsheet program, such as Microsoft Excel, makes it easy to sort your client list in different ways for different mailings. Flag your clients so that you can see their real estate interests. Are they homebuyers or sellers, people who bought or are interested in land, investors, or commercial buyers or sellers?

You can also develop special marketing packages for the different categories of clients. If they just bought or sold a house—maybe both—they aren't likely in the market for a new one yet. You won't need to send those people flyers about your current listings, but you'll definitely want to add them to your holiday card list and make sure they receive mailings from you on a regular basis. At the anniversary of their purchase, send a card or a simple gift and congratulate them on their first year in the home. Even clients who have sold and moved away may still have contacts in their old neighborhood. They are a great source of referrals if you stay connected. Mailings are not enough though—be sure to call these people periodically. Ask them if they need anything and, if they do, follow through and take care of their needs. Whether or not they have a need, be sure to thank them for their business and ask them for referrals.

## Question

**What types of mailings are suitable for someone who just bought a house?**

How about a postcard in the fall that offers suggestions for home and garden winterization tasks, like checking the chimney and covering roses? A spring mailing could focus on spring-cleaning and organizing.

Investors are people whom you should stay in contact with on a regular basis. Mail or e-mail information to them as new properties come on the market. Design your mailings to suit each specific group of people who will receive them.

### Referrals

Always tell your past clients that you appreciate any referrals they can give you. Most people don't remember to do this unless you remind them in person or in a special mailing. Send out at least one mailing each year that specifically asks your past clients for referrals. If you send out monthly or quarterly mailings, insert a short statement in each one that lets people know you appreciate their referral business. Follow up your mailers with phone calls for greater impact.

### Written Testimonials

People tend to put things in writing more often when they're unhappy about a person or service than they do when they're pleased. Keep that in mind when dealing with your clients, because they won't normally give you written endorsements unless you ask for them.

Put one or two short, written recommendations from satisfied selling clients in your listing presentation. Insert buyer testimonials in a resume you prepare for new buyer clients. Many agents use client testimonials on their Web sites. Recommendations from others make a powerful statement to new clients that you are the agent who can get the job done for them.

## *If Things Don't Go Well*

Even the most honest person in the world can get into trouble if he or she does not know the law and does not properly apply it. Knowing all the rules and regulations tied to real estate will protect you from inadvertently doing something wrong. As obvious as it seems, start with honesty in all dealings and be sure that everything is in writing.

Sometimes, knowing the law isn't enough to keep you out of trouble. Complaints from one party or the other, either legitimate or picky, will need to be settled. You'll be required to use your best negotiation skills to eliminate the complaints and keep them from becoming lawsuits. In some cases, problems can arise that affect all parties, and you are the one expected to solve them.

Still, it happens every day—unhappy customers and clients file lawsuits and report real estate agents to their state licensing commissions. You must make an effort to conduct your business in a way that helps ensure that no one will make a complaint against you, but that isn't enough. It's essential to take steps to defend yourself against frivolous complaints and complaints that result when you truly do make an error in your work.

### Common Complaints

The three most important words in real estate for a buyer or a seller are *location, location, location*. For an agent, it is *disclosure, disclosure, disclosure*. Disclosures need to be in writing, most of them on a form specific to the real estate division in your state. Disclosure number one is the agency disclosure. As a real estate agent, it is essential that you disclose your agency relationship, whom you work for, in every transaction. This disclosure must be made *up front*.

## E Alert

Keep a log in your client file of all phone calls relating to that transaction. Note the date and time of each call, whom you spoke with, and what was discussed. Used consistently, this log can keep you out of trouble. It is wise to print all e-mails and add them to the file as well.

You may be working for the seller, either as a listing agent or as a subagent through the MLS. If this is the case, you must disclose it to the buyer. The buyer must have the opportunity to decide if she wants her own representation. If you are working for the buyer, this fact must also be disclosed. Although compensation traditionally comes from the seller's proceeds, this is not always the case. Some buyers will pay to have representation, such as in the purchase of a for sale by owner. Compensation does not always mean representation. It is possible to represent the buyer even if your compensation comes from the seller.

If you are working for both parties as a dual agent, this disclosure must also be made. Both parties have the right to decide if they want you to work as a dual agent. If one or the other, or both parties, do not want to have an agent who is representing everyone, either the buyer or the seller must be assigned to someone else.

Disclosure number two is whether you are a party to the real estate transaction. If you are the buyer or the seller in a real estate transaction, or if you are related to the buyer or the seller, this fact must be disclosed. Even if the buyer or seller is a corporation, and you are a minor stockholder of the corporation, this must be disclosed. Even if your name does not appear as the buyer or seller, if you receive a benefit over and above the benefit of your commission, it must be made known to all parties.

Disclosure number three includes everything else:

- Common interest communities (such as condominiums, townhouses, or cooperatives)
- By-laws
- Rules and regulations
- Dues, assessments, budget, and reserves
- Recent minutes of association meetings
- Stigmatized properties
- Location of new developments
- Location of nearby ranch lands
- Related to the inspector, lender, or other party to the transaction
- Agent or company receives compensation from someone else in the transaction. For example: if the insurance company sponsors the office Christmas party or a bonus or gift is presented to the agent by a particular pest inspector for every referral she provides.
- Office is affiliated with other offices that provide related services such as lenders, title, or escrow.
- Lead paint, hazardous materials, radon, mold

If in doubt, disclose. It is better to disclose more than necessary than to find yourself faced with a lawsuit for lack of disclosure.

## Essential Records

Every area of the country is different and there are different requirements as to what you need to include in a file. Check first with your broker and find out what her requirements are. Your broker should know what forms the state and the local municipalities require.

If your office is part of a franchise, there may also be special forms that they require. From there, check with your state's division of real estate to be sure that your broker did not miss anything and that there are not any new requirements. You may also wish to check with a real estate attorney, especially if you work in a state where attorneys handle the closings.

## Question

**Do I have to have signatures on all the documents?**

Yes. A contract is not binding without all the signatures. Be sure that every form is signed by all parties. Some states allow signatures in counterpart (on two separate copies of the same form); others do not.

Make a checklist of required forms and continue to expand on it, depending on the requirements of your state, of your office, and of your local municipalities. Because real estate is constantly changing, new and different forms may be required on a regular basis. Be sure you are aware of any changes in regulations and keep your list of required forms current.

Here is a preliminary list of key documents:

1. Purchase agreement or offer and acceptance
2. Any counteroffers
3. Addendums
4. Agency disclosures
5. Common interest community disclosures
6. Lead paint disclosure (if built before 1978)
7. Other disclosures
8. Copy of inspection reports
9. Copy of pest report
10. Copy of repair bills
11. Escrow instructions (for states with escrow)
12. Copies of attorney's paperwork (for states where attorneys handle closings)
13. Copy of seller's disclosure statement
14. Preliminary title report
15. Closing statement
16. Phone log/e-mail log

Your state laws dictate which official transaction documents you must keep and how long you must keep them, but your complete records should contain more than the signed contracts and other forms required by the state.

Take notes during your discussions with clients, especially when you're talking about problem issues such as repairs. Record dates and times and make sure to write down whether you had a telephone conversation or a face-to-face meeting. If you're a listing agent, keep all documents associated with measuring a structure's square footage.

## Essential

Make a checklist of all the necessary forms and keep copies of the list. Add the list to the front of every new file and use it to avoid forgetting any required forms.

There are times you should consider asking your client to sign a statement that she made a decision about the transaction against your advice. Maybe the client refused to have a pest inspection or radon test, even though you recommended both. Keeping a document in your files where she verified in writing that not performing those inspections was her choice will help you tremendously if she finds an active termite infestation or high levels of radon gas after moving in.

Keep records of your conversations with other real estate professionals who are associated with the transaction, such as appraisers, mortgage people, home inspectors, and others. Make your records as detailed as possible. Written documentation about a past event can be an effective tool if someone files a complaint about the role you played in a real estate transaction.

## *Working Through the Problem*

A complaint that affects you might not even be about you. Sometimes buyers and sellers are unhappy with each other and file complaints against every real estate professional involved in a transaction, in hopes that someone will step in and fix their problems—usually by paying for a repair or another expense associated with the sale.

When you are in the throes of a transaction it is easy to think solely about your client's needs, even to the detriment of the other party. You want to *win* and you don't care if that means the other person loses. This can make any problems that arise difficult to sort out. Consider this scenario:

A buyer sees a house that she wants to purchase. The buyer's agent presents the offer to the seller and his agent by saying, "This buyer really loves your house. She is offering you $185,000, just $4,000 less than your asking price of $189,000 because she really wants you to consider accepting her offer." The inspections are completed and although there are a lot of very little, almost nitpicky items, there is only one major item that needs repair. The glass shower enclosure in the bathroom is cracked. The buyer's agent counsels his buyer to be reasonable and ask only for the major repair item. He then approaches the seller's agent with a request to fix the shower enclosure, stating that none of the other items are important to the buyer because she knows the seller gave her such a fair price. The deal closes and everyone is happy.

A month later, the buyer discovers mold. She is very upset and talks to her agent about suing the seller for nondisclosure. The buyer's agent does not convey how upset his buyer is. He goes to the seller's agent and explains that mold was found. He says he knows that the seller was reasonable throughout the process and asks him to be reasonable now. The seller is more likely to take care of the problem as he had a smooth and easy transaction with the buyer. He likes the buyer, even if he never met her.

Consider this scenario with a twist. The buyer's agent presents the offer and says, "These buyers think you are overpriced so they are only offering $185,000 instead of the $189,000 you are asking." When the inspections come the buyer asks for every little nitpicky item. When the mold is found, how do you think the seller will react? He doesn't like the buyer, and he may sue his real estate agent for not disclosing that a mold test was necessary. More likely than suing only his agent, the seller will sue everyone and let the courts sort out who is responsible. Win or lose, a lawsuit takes time and money and can cost you your reputation.

## Errors and Omissions Insurance Protection

Just as a doctor should have medical malpractice insurance, a real estate agent should have errors and omissions insurance. This insurance protects you against a lawsuit if you inadvertently make a mistake. The operative word here is inadvertently. If you purposely commit fraud or negligence, your insurance company may not cover you.

### E Alert

It is important to add your real estate office to your automobile insurance policy as an additional insured. If you are in an accident with a client or customer in the car, you and your office can be held liable for any injuries that person sustains.

Some clients will file a lawsuit against you in hopes of receiving money for the damages they believe you caused. Even if you make no mistakes on the job, there are always people who attempt to sue others for invalid or frivolous reasons. The fact is, everyone makes a mistake some time during his career. No matter who wins in court, your legal expenses must be paid. E&O insurance can help.

Common E&O coverage includes claims that result from errors, omissions, or negligence during your work as a real estate agent. Exclusions (things the insurance company will not pay for) usually include:

- Claims that result from dishonesty or when you've committed a criminal act
- Claims regarding your knowledge of pollution on a property
- Claims against you if you injure or kill someone
- Claims against you when you've damaged a property

Like your auto and homeowners insurance, E&O policies have a deductible—a specified amount you must pay before the insurance coverage kicks in. Some E&O policies have two deductibles, one for defense costs and one for damages.

## Essential

You should ask your insurance agent to check your auto liability coverage. You probably need to increase your coverage now that you're an agent who transports people on a regular basis. Your insurance agent might need to put you into a different category for that coverage.

Your real estate firm might have an E&O policy that protects its agents. Ask your broker-in-charge for that information, then take the details to your own insurance professional to make sure the coverage is adequate for your needs. If your insurance agent doesn't handle that type of coverage, ask for a referral to a company that does.

## *Minimizing Your Risk*

Your best defense against a lawsuit is to know the law. Many of the mistakes made by real estate agents are made because the agent was not aware that she was doing something incorrectly, or (more often) not doing something she was supposed to do. The more informed you are, the less likely you are to make a mistake. Not knowing the law is not considered an excuse. You are the professional and you are expected to know.

You are also expected to know things that are considered "public knowledge." Let's say that a new community is planned for the open space behind the house you are selling. Although the sellers have enjoyed peace and quiet and the view of green rolling hills for a long time, this will be changing soon. It has been in all the papers and the developers have even held a public meeting to answer questions that the neighbors have. You need to disclose this fact to any prospective purchaser. Chances are this information is in the seller's disclosure, but what if the seller moved away from the community years ago and a tenant lives in the property? What if it is vacant? No matter whether or not the seller discloses this fact, it is still "public knowledge," and you are expected to know it and to disclose it.

A thorough understanding of the state real estate laws that affect agents is a major step toward minimizing your risk of valid complaints. All agents learn these laws in prelicensing school, but it's easy to forget the intricacies of the laws once they have moved beyond the test-cramming tactics that most people employ to pass the state exam. There are several things you can do to stay current with laws:

- Pay attention during your required continuing-education updates.
- Take additional continuing-education classes each year—more than the required hours.
- Don't miss educational classes presented by your local MLS, because they usually deal with risk management and ethics, two top complaint-related issues.
- Take time to read updated booklets or flyers from your state licensing commission.
- Monitor your real estate commission's Web site if it includes updates to laws that affect you.

You cannot prevent unhappy clients from lodging a complaint against you, but you can do your best to make sure you have complied with all state real estate laws, making it less likely that a complaint will result in the loss of your license.

### Fact

Your local Board of Realtors® can fine you or request that you beef up your education if a committee of your peers determines that you acted improperly during a transaction, but only your state licensing commission can take away your real estate license.

Even if you make an honest error, you may be able to avoid a lawsuit by the manner in which you handled the transaction from the start. Keeping good records, being honest in all dealings, disclosing all material facts, including all ways that you receive compensation in the transaction, will go a long way toward minimizing your risks.

Be up-front and noncombative with all parties, look for solutions, and handle everything calmly and without finger-pointing. Conducting yourself this way will decrease the chance of someone getting upset with you—even if things go wrong. Apologies and graciousness can help to keep you out of court.

## Proper Handling of Money

Improper handling of money is among the most common reasons an agent gets into trouble. If your office handles earnest money deposits through their trust account, the proper accounting of those funds is critical. It is also important to tell the truth regarding whether or not there is an earnest money deposit. Perhaps your client promised it to you but did not have his checkbook with him. Even if you are expecting it momentarily, you must disclose that you do not have the deposit in your account.

Conspiracy is a word that sounds terribly ominous. Many agents have unwittingly entered into a conspiracy without even realizing it. Imagine your buyer wants to purchase a house for $250,000 and the seller is willing to sell it to them for that amount. Say the buyer does not have any money for a down payment so she decides to offer $300,000, to get the loan for $250,000 but not actually pay $300,000. If you agree to this type of contract you are entering into a conspiracy to defraud the lender. Chances are if an action feels wrong or it sounds wrong, it is wrong.

## Discrimination

The U.S. Department of Housing and Urban Development (HUD) has very strict guidelines against discrimination. You may not even think you are being discriminatory, but if language you use either in person or in print indicates that you are, you may be held liable. You may not say, "There are a lot of (insert name of ethnic group or age group) in this neighborhood, so you'll feel comfortable here." You may not steer people to and from neighborhoods based on their similarities or differences with the other residents of the neighborhood.

### E Alert

Title VIII of the Civil Rights Act of 1968 (Fair Housing Act), as amended, prohibits discrimination in the sale, rental, and financing of dwellings, and in other housing-related transactions, based on race, color, national origin, religion, sex, familial status, and handicap (disability).

It is possible to be brought up on discrimination charges if you treat one group of people "differently" from another. If, for example, you always offer coffee to people who come to your office but you fail to offer coffee to a person in a wheelchair, this may be considered discriminatory. If you immediately take out a couple who are of the same race to see property but only give a list of potential properties to a mixed race couple and let them drive around, this can be considered discriminatory as well.

To be sure that you are not acting in a discriminatory manner, you can learn more on the HUD Web site at *www.hud.gov* or by seeing if your office has a HUD guidelines handout.

## *RESPA*

The other area that may lead you into trouble is noncompliance with RESPA laws. RESPA is the Real Estate Settlement Procedures Act, which designates how a lender or title company can provide benefit to real estate agents. In general you may not accept contributions or gifts from title companies or lenders. The rules are too complicated and ever-changing to completely outline here, but you may learn more about RESPA at *www.realtor.org/RESPA* or at the RESPA section of the Housing and Urban Development Web site at *www.hud.gov/offices/hsg/sfh/res/respa_hm.cfm.*

Chances are, most transactions will be a positive experience for all parties involved and after the sale you will be fielding questions and helping your clients settle in. You will be receiving referrals and taking time to thank the people you have been working with. Sometimes there will be glitches. By practicing full disclosure and full documentation, keeping good financial records, treating everyone honestly, and by not acting in a discriminatory manner, you can keep glitches from becoming lawsuits. More important, these behaviors are the keys to good business practice and by using them, you will build a reputation that continues to generate new and repeat business.

Chapter 15

# Managing Your Finances

**The most important** thing to remember about managing your finances is this: As a real estate agent, you no longer have a job—you are now a business owner. Managing your finances is more than just putting your paycheck in the bank and paying your bills. Managing your finances now includes running your business, preferably at a profit. As a business owner, only a portion of each check can be considered income that is yours to keep. You will need to pay your taxes and expenses before you pay yourself.

## *Income Projections*

Homebuyers and sellers often assume that the entire commission paid to sell real estate goes to one agent, but that's not how it works. Real estate commissions are nearly always shared by all of the agencies that participate in a sale.

**Essential**

Self-employed real estate agents are responsible for managing their income potential and outgoing expenses—and reporting both to the Internal Revenue Service.

The buyer's closing agent is responsible for paying every person who is due funds at the end of a transaction, and the list of recipients includes the real estate firms that participated. Payments are made to firms, not to individual agents.

Commissions are usually paid from the seller's proceeds and are calculated as a percentage of the total sales price. If you belong to a multiple listing service, the percentage your office will receive for a sale should be shown on each MLS fact sheet.

The information might be encoded in a field with initials such as "BAC," which stands for buyer agency commission. If that field says "3," you'll know that your firm will receive a check for 3 percent of the sales price if you sell the property while acting as a buyer's agent. The field "SAC" indicates how much you'll receive when working as a seller's agent or seller's subagent, both of which describe agents who are *not* contracted to work as a buyer's agent.

**Fact**

If you acted as a buyer's agent to sell an unlisted property, your commission payment would come from your buyer and the seller would not pay a commission. Buyer agency contracts cover compensation issues for that scenario and others.

In many states the seller's subagency commission will be lower, if any exists at all. Listing agents do not often want a subagent to represent their seller. They may feel the subagent does not *know* their seller or have their seller's best interests at heart. Your MLS might use different wording or coding to display the commission information, especially if your state laws define agent/buyer relationships in another way. Check with your supervising broker to learn how to read your MLS sheets.

### How Commissions Are Split

Commissions are usually split equally between the listing and selling offices, but variations sometimes occur. For example, one office might have agreed to lower its commission in order to help the buyers and sellers negotiate a contract. Sometimes an agency takes a listing for a lesser percentage than it normally charges and offers selling firms more than half of the total to entice them to show the property. Each half of the transaction is known as a *side*. If you sell your own listing you would receive *two sides*, or both halves, of the commission.

There is no "set" or "standard" commission percentage charged by real estate firms—that would be illegal. Each firm decides how much commission to charge for its services. It is common to see similar commissions charged by many firms within an area, as agencies compete with each other for listings.

### The Franchising Company's Share

A firm affiliated with a franchising corporation, such as Century 21, Prudential, or ERA, typically pays the corporation a percentage of each commission check. This percentage is usually in the range of 6 to 8 percent and is likely just one of the fees the firm pays to keep the franchise. The deduction comes out of the total amount received by the firm, reducing your net commission. There are independent offices that also charge a fee. They call it an advertising fee, but it is often in the same percentage range as a franchise's fee.

### Calculating Your Commission

It's easy to calculate how much commission you will earn from a sale. Let's say you worked with a buyer and sold a house for $100,000. Assuming that you were offered a 3 percent commission through the multiple listing service, 3 percent of the sales amount is paid to your real estate firm: $100,000 × .03, for a total of $3,000. Assuming that your firm pays you 50 percent of the commissions your work produces: $3,000 × .50, or $1,500.

**E Alert**

> Some agents pay firms a monthly fee for office space and brokerage services. These agents keep all of the commission earned from their closings, instead of sharing a percentage with the firm. Monthly fees are usually hefty, so that type of arrangement isn't usually suitable for agents who don't have a consistent income.

If you work for a franchised agency, your commission check might include a deduction for your portion of the payment that will be sent to the franchising corporation. If that fee is 8 percent, it would affect your income like this:

$3,000 paid to firm × .08 = $240 franchise fee, or $2,760 base pay
$2,760 × .50 split = $1,380 payment to you

If you listed and sold the same property, the amount of commission paid to your firm would double, and so would your pay. This paycheck is considered gross income and you will be responsible for paying your taxes out of that amount. So, when you figure out the payment that comes to you, you must remember that not all of it is yours.

### Commission Variations

Many real estate firms offer agents an incentive by paying commissions on a sliding scale, with the percentage increasing as agents bring more revenue to the agency. Rates are typically reset to the lowest percentage annually, or on the anniversary of the date you started with the firm. Each year, you'll work your way back up to the higher bracket.

**Fact**

Many agents make more than 50 percent of the commissions they bring to a firm. That figure is only an example. You'll have an opportunity to negotiate a commission split when you interview for a position with an agency.

Some firms pay agents a higher percentage of the commissions received if the sale is an "in-house" transaction, meaning one that occurs when both the listing and selling agents work for the same firm. Because the agency doesn't share the commission with another firm, it rewards its agents by paying them a higher commission. This is often known as a "variable rate commission," and must be disclosed in the multiple listing information.

Sit down with a pencil and paper and try a few commission calculations. You'll see how easy it is. Once you go to work, you'll be ready to check your commission statements for accuracy.

## Setting Financial Goals

How much money do you want to make? Start by writing three financial goals: a short-term goal, a midrange goal, and a long-term goal. Your goals should be specific and have a time frame attached to them. The short-term goal is what you expect to accomplish within the next few months, the midrange goal is what you expect to accomplish within the next year, and the long-term goal can be a projection of three or more years. They may look something like this:

**Short term:** Make a total commission of $10,000 by my three-month anniversary.

**Midrange:** Make a total commission of $36,000 by my one-year anniversary.

**Long term:** Make a commission of $100,000 per year and hire an assistant by my three-year anniversary.

Once you have set the goals, place them on your desk or on your mirror and read them every day.

## Income Realities

How many houses do you need to sell in order to make your financial goals? Start by figuring out the average sales price in your area and the average commission being offered. Assuming that you receive a 60 percent commission split, your income projection would look like this:

| | |
|---|---|
| Average sales price | $200,000 |
| Average commission offered | $6,000 |
| Less the office's share of 40 percent | $2,400 |
| Gross to agent of 60 percent | $3,600 |
| Less taxes of 30 percent | $1,080 |
| Net to agent | $2,520 |
| Less expenses | $350 |
| Amount to live on | $2,170 |

It is important to know that new agents usually start out selling property in the lower-than-average price range, so you may want to be more conservative with your average sales price figure.

## *Your Tax Responsibilities*

One of the first things you'll notice when you receive a check is that absolutely no taxes have been deducted from it. You are self-employed and responsible for reporting your income and paying all taxes due for the money you earn. Your real estate firm will give you and the IRS a 1099-Miscellaneous form each year that shows how much you earned during the previous tax year.

The form of your business plays a role in your tax situation. A certified public accountant (CPA) can help you determine the most effective way to structure your business. Your options include sole proprietorship, partnership, C-Corporation, S-Corporation, or Limited Liability Company.

### Sole Proprietorship

Sole proprietorship is the most simple and commonly used form of ownership for independent contractors. There are no forms to complete; you simply state that you are a sole proprietor and report your income and expenses using IRS Form 1040 Schedule C. You, as the owner of your sole proprietorship, are personally responsible for all debts and actions.

## Partnership

A partnership occurs when at least two people decide to go into business together and do not apply to become a type of corporation. Each individual partner is responsible for their own as well as the other partner's debts and actions.

### Question

**As an individual agent, can you choose an entity other than sole proprietorship?**

Check with your state division of real estate. Some states will only allow payment to the individual who has the real estate license and will not allow your commission to be paid to a corporation or an LLC, as they do not allow you to limit your liability in any way.

## Corporation or C-Corporation

A corporation or C-Corporation is a legal entity that is registered with a state secretary and recognized by the IRS as the taxpayer for your business. The corporation can hold title to property and do many of the same things a person can, but its members are not typically personally liable for corporation debts. All debts are paid by the C-Corporation and a salary is paid to the shareholders. There is a potential double taxation, once at the corporate level and once at the shareholder level. The corporation is first subject to tax at the corporate level, and then any profits (or dividends) the corporation distributes to the shareholders are subject to tax as well. This type of corporation is often used for offices but rarely used for individual agents.

## S-Corporation

Many independent contractors are opting for this business classification because it can offer significant tax savings. Your commission payments are made to the S-Corporation and the corporation pays you a salary. Any profits are also passed through to you as a shareholder and thus only taxed once.

### Limited Liability Company (LLC)

A Limited Liability Company (LLC) is a legal entity that is easier and less expensive to organize and run than a corporation, but offers its members some of the same benefits, including personal liability protection.

Creating any type of corporate entity requires filling out forms and registering your business with your secretary of state. Make an appointment to consult with a CPA to determine which form of business best suits your needs. Once you decide, an attorney or CPA can also help you with the initial setup.

## *Tax Deductions and Payments*

Nearly every expense associated with your job is a tax-deductible expense, meaning that it is a cost that lowers your claimed income—and, as a result, lowers your taxes. Even little expenses add up over time, so save receipts for any expense related to your real estate career. Filling out your forms when tax day arrives is much easier if you've kept good records all year long.

**Fact**

Real estate agents commonly get behind on their taxes from the beginning of their careers. Because they do not have taxes taken from their check and because they do not know how much their income will be, they have a tendency to underreport and hope for a big closing in time to pay the IRS in April.

Accurate records help you monitor the progress of your business and they'll come in handy if the Internal Revenue Service ever audits your tax return. When you're audited, the IRS might ask to see proof of when an expense occurred and how it is connected to your business. The more answers you provide, the easier it is to substantiate your claim that costs are truly business related.

Some of your expenses will include:

- Advertising costs
- Auto expenses, for upkeep and miles driven
- Office supplies
- Postage and delivery
- Dues paid to business organizations
- Client gifts
- Education and training expenses
- Licensing fees
- Business travel expenses
- Entertainment (within IRS limits)
- Insurance
- Equipment
- Professional advice (attorney, CPA, tax professional)
- Payments to assistants
- Rent for office space
- Office space in your home

If an expense is related to your work, it is probably tax deductible. Your tax professional can help you determine which of your costs are valid business expenses.

### Essential

Instead of being deducted in one large chunk in a single year, the costs of expensive items with multiyear lives (such as computer equipment and furniture) are spread out over several years. This process is called depreciation.

The expense for your home office can create a major tax deduction in some cases. If you have an office in an office building, as well as a home office, your home office may not be deductible at all. Laws change periodically, so discuss home office requirements with your tax professional and be sure to follow IRS guidelines when you set up and manage a home office.

### Making Tax Payments

Employers deduct a certain percentage of taxes from each employee paycheck and submit the funds to federal, state, and local governments as required so that by the end of the year the employee has prepaid the majority of his taxes. As a self-employed real estate agent, that is no longer done for you, so you must make periodic estimated tax payments yourself.

Plan to begin submitting monthly or quarterly tax payments when your real estate income begins. It's a lot easier to set aside and pay small portions with single checks than it is to come up with a huge chunk of money on tax day. You might also be fined for underpayment if the IRS determines you should have submitted taxes on a quarterly basis and didn't.

### Helpful Software Programs

There are excellent, intuitive software programs available for people who feel comfortable preparing their own tax returns. TurboTax is a program that has been around for many years and is easy to use. You can import your computer-generated financial information into TurboTax to speed up your return and eliminate errors that occur when transferring data by hand.

## Question

**How can I learn more about taxes and accounting?**
Ask if your local community college offers classes for either subject. Inquire at nearby franchised tax offices, such as H&R Block, to find out when and where their annual training classes are held.

## Business vs. Personal Checking

As a self-employed individual, you should open a business checking account. Every dollar of commission earned should go through this account first. This is the account you will use to pay all your real estate related expenses. You will need to make tax payments to the IRS from this account as well.

You will not know what tax bracket you are going to be in when you first start in real estate, but you do know that you will be paying self-employment tax. Self-employment tax is the employer and employee shares that are due to the Social Security system and Medicare. Normally the employer is required to pay part of this tax and the employee pays the rest. Because you are self-employed, you must pay both shares. This cost may change annually, but is currently at 15.3 percent. Check with *www.irs.gov* for the most up-to-date information.

If you assume that you will be in one of the lower tax brackets the first year you are in the business, you can take approximately one-third of each commission check and set it aside for the IRS. Deposit this money in a separate savings account to keep from spending it, and use it to make the quarterly payments. Your tax advisor can show you how to set up a quarterly payment plan with the IRS.

### E Alert

If you don't make quarterly payments, you may be responsible for hefty penalties and interest when your annual taxes come due. If you receive a hefty commission check, you may actually need to deposit more often than quarterly, so be sure your tax advisor knows if you receive an unusually high commission.

Once you have paid toward your taxes and paid all your business expenses, you can write yourself a check to deposit in your personal account. Keep some money in your business account for ongoing expenses, in case you do not have any commissions forthcoming.

After the first quarterly payment, you and your CPA can determine if you are on track or behind for the year. If you are ahead, don't be tempted to spend the money. Chances are your business will continue to improve, and it is better to have money set aside than to try and find it later.

### Your Automobile

It's essential to keep track of the number of miles you put on your car to conduct business. Some agents take a per-mile tax deduction and others opt to use actual auto expenses as their deduction, but both groups of agents record their business miles to determine which method is best and to help them calculate the percentages of business and personal use.

#### Fact

Most people are so computer oriented now that many agents use electronic log and appointment books to record their mileage and daily tasks. Use the method that suits you best, but talk to a tax professional to find out what type of permanent records the IRS requires if an audit takes place.

Record your odometer reading at the beginning of the tax year—for most of us that is January 1. Keep a mileage log in your car and enter a date and location for each beginning odometer reading, both business and personal. Record the date and time when that particular use ends. For business use, and an even more complete record, jot down the name of the client you were with. Use a bright highlighter to mark your business trips so they are more visible. Total your business and personal miles each week or month.

### Written Receipts

The IRS will not always accept a canceled check or a credit card statement as verification of an expense. You must keep the actual receipts for your expenses in order to prove exactly what you purchased. Keeping all of your receipts for the required three years (sometimes longer) can generate a mountain of paperwork that is impossible to dig through if you don't keep it organized.

When you buy something with a credit card, staple individual receipts to the statement when it arrives so that all documents related to the sale are in the same place. Most banks don't return canceled checks anymore, but they do normally provide you with copies of the checks. Attach all receipts that are associated with your checks and deposits to the appropriate statement. Cluster all cash receipts together and arrange them by date in another file.

Keep an ongoing log of your expenses by date. A program, such as Quicken or Microsoft Money, works like a checkbook but lets you enter and categorize all outgoing and incoming funds, whether they are by paid by check, credit card, or cash. You can use the search features in the program to quickly find a transaction by name, date, or category. Once you know how and when you purchased the item, it's easy to retrieve the receipts from your files.

**E Alert**

Some tax professionals recommend that you keep all of your receipts, both business and personal, so that you can show the division between the two types of expenses. Ask your own tax person for advice on which records you should keep.

When the tax year ends, gather all of the current year's records into a storage box, mark the year on the outside, and put the box in a safe location until it can be legally disposed of.

## *Managing Your Expenses*

There are many ways to spend money as a real estate agent. You need a decent car, nice clothing, and good promotional materials. You want a quality Web site that can be found on all the search engines, and you have the costs of education, desk rent, phone, computer, and supplies. All of these expenses can end up taking their toll on your actual income.

Create a budget for your business. Of course, this is hard to do if you do not know how much money is coming in. Think of your business expenses the same way you think of your mortgage; you have to pay it even if you don't have money coming in.

Find out the costs of the promotional material you will need, the costs of postage and other expenses, and create a spreadsheet. Some costs will not occur monthly but they should be in your monthly budget. If you do not need a new car right now but hope to get one in the future, start budgeting for it right away. Because technology changes daily, it is also a good idea to set aside money each month toward a new computer, even if you have one now that works just fine.

Start with a list of the expenses you anticipate. This list will give you a place to start:

- Business cards
- Professional photo
- Newspaper ads
- Glossy magazine ads
- Other ads
- Flyers and brochures
- Mailers
- Postage
- Automobile and automobile expenses
- Clothing and dry-cleaning expenses
- Education
- Computer, software, Web design and hosting
- Cell phone and airtime costs
- Keys and lockboxes
- Signs, sign riders, and brochure boxes
- MLS dues and other fees
- E&O insurance and other insurances
- Client gifts

Think of ways that you can save money, because chances are there will be unforeseen expenses, too. Can one of your friends or your family members take a good photo of you to save the cost of a professional photo? Can you deliver mailers to your farm area to save on postage, knocking on doors and leaving items on the doorstep if no one is home? Can you create professional flyers on your computer or is there an office supply store that can make inexpensive color copies for you? Will a smaller ad with an interesting border have as much impact as a larger ad in the local paper? Your budget will change as you learn what works best in your market and where you can save money, as well as what additional costs you will need to consider.

## Essential

A good rule of thumb for marketing costs on your listings is 8 to 15 percent of the commission you will receive. Lower-priced properties will be less expensive to advertise as they usually sell more quickly than the higher-priced properties. Overpriced properties cost the most to market, since they take the longest amount of time to sell.

Think about your budget as each new expense comes up. If you ended up with more listings than you expected and need to increase the flyer budget, try to take the money from another source in your budget (but not from your money set aside for the IRS). If it is something that can wait, such as paying to be the only agent in your area to be referred by a certain Web site, then wait until your budget can be expanded.

If you are worried about money, you will seem desperate when you are meeting with clients. By keeping track of your finances and budgeting you will be able to relax about money and focus on taking care of your clients and customers instead of concentrating on your financial concerns.

Chapter 16

# The World Wide Web

**The majority of** full-time real estate agents now have Web sites to provide prospective clients with information about themselves or their listings. Internet exposure offers agents a relatively inexpensive way to inform consumers seven days a week, twenty-four hours a day. Obtaining a Web site isn't difficult at all, but agents do have many decisions to make before they jump in to the Internet community.

## *Choosing and Registering a Domain Name*

Internet users have spent years now devising clever and useful domain names for their businesses, so finding a domain name that hasn't already been registered for use is sometimes not an easy task. With a little brainstorming, you can devise a name that suits your new business perfectly.

A uniform resource locator, which is called *URL* for short, is the address of an individual page on the World Wide Web. If you use the Web, you recognize the URL as the long string of characters that is automatically entered in the address line of an Internet browser, such as Netscape, Internet Explorer, or Safari, when you click on a link. You can also type the address in the opening and hit "Go," or press the return key on your keyboard to access the page.

Your domain name is the portion of the URL that typically comes after *www* and before *.com*—or *.net, .org, .biz,* and other common endings. Like this:

*www.**yourdomain**.com*

Domain names can be registered through one of many accredited registrars (companies approved to conduct that type of business for Web users). Some registrars act solely as a registering agent, but many others offer to provide you with a place to host your Web site so that people can see it. Domain names can be registered for periods ranging from one to ten years. Registration fees vary depending on the registering company and the length of time you choose to register the name.

## Essential

ICANN, the Internet Corporation for Assigned Names and Numbers, is a nonprofit corporation that coordinates several Internet functions. One of its responsibilities is to oversee the domain name system. Learn about ICANN at *www.ican.org.*

Many real estate agents register and use their personal names for their real estate domain name and, in fact, Internet savvy businesspeople suggest that everyone register his or her name, even if they have no immediate plans to use it, because registration blocks anyone else from obtaining it. No matter how many agencies you work for, your name is the one constant that people who know you will recognize. If you have a common name, it may already be registered. If that is the case, try using a portion of your name to create a phrase, like gloriasellshomes.com.

You might prefer to choose a domain name that ties in with your location or the type of business you do. Most town and city names have already been registered, but it's not too difficult to work something into your domain name that relates to your town name or to something unique about your location. Think about your local attractions. Can you think of a descriptive term associated with the area to use in your name?

If you plan to advertise your Web site address in newspapers and magazines, try to keep your domain name as short and catchy as possible so that people remember it. Avoid using hyphens and other symbols that people might not remember to type in.

If you marry and change your name or change your name for other reasons, you can register your new name and configure the old Web site to link to the new.

## *Developing Your Web Site*

The type of Web site you choose depends on your expertise and the amount of time you plan to spend updating it yourself. Do you have time to design the pages from scratch and keep listing up-to-date information? Would you rather use a system that streamlines the process for you? You can choose either route, with several variables in between.

There are numerous networks (companies with servers, which are large computers, that connect all of the computers linked in a network) that offer predesigned real estate Web sites and hosting; that is, they store the pages so they can be accessed on the Web. These networks usually have a large selection of designs to choose from. These designs are called *templates*, a kind of skeleton page that looks pretty but has no text. The templates make creating your Web page as simple as typing your name and other data into specific slots and hitting a "save" button on the screen. Your information flows to the right parts of the template to complete the design.

You can usually choose the text style (font) you like best, and can often vary its size and color. The design process is very intuitive, so you don't need any former Internet experience to end up with a professional-looking Web site.

### Fact

You can search for available domain names at *www.networksolutions.com*. That company will register your chosen name for you. It also offers many types of Web site hosting packages.

Most network portals have a maximum allowable size for photos that can be uploaded to the Internet. (*Uploading* is the name used to describe the transfer of digital images or other files from your computer to a Web site.) You'll want your photos to be as large as possible for best visibility, so be sure to compare maximum photo sizes when you compare networks. Bigger files take longer for people to *download*, the term used for viewing, so find a size that looks good but still downloads quickly.

Many of the Internet-based MLS services also provide a Web site for their members. This site may be a great place to start if you want to keep the process as simple as possible.

If you're still working with printed photos, rather than digital images, plan to pay extra for the hosting company to scan them and put them online for you. The costs for that service are high enough to pay for a digital camera in no time, so start looking for a camera that suits your needs (see Chapter 10). If you have access to a scanner, you have the ability to convert your printed photos to digital images on your own. You can submit the images to your Web-hosting company via e-mail, but be sure to get details about the size and resolution they require before you scan.

## Essential

There are networks that specialize in designing unique Web sites for their real estate clients, instead of asking you to choose from preformatted versions. A higher level of design work by someone else creates more expense for you, but the end result might be worth it.

Cost for network space varies greatly depending on the hosting company you choose, and unless your MLS has an arrangement with the company to feed data into it regularly, you are responsible for keeping the information on your Web site current. Updates aren't difficult but they're something you must remember to do when you sell a listing, change a price, or make any other alterations to one of your properties. You may actually be violating state laws if you do not remove sold properties or otherwise keep your Web site current.

## *Building a Web Site from Scratch*

Designing and building a Web site yourself is usually the least expensive way to get on the Internet, but it requires time and a bit more expertise. Doing it yourself will be easiest if you already understand how to code a Web site using online programming language. However, there are software programs to help even if you only have a minimal understanding of the methods.

If you are creating your own Web site, you will design and save all of your files on your own computer, then upload them to storage space on the Web that's been configured to match your domain name. Every time you have a change, you will edit the incorrect page stored on your computer and upload it again. This step overwrites and replaces the outdated page, as long as you keep file names identical.

There are special software programs for people who aren't familiar with Web programming that look and work a lot like the word processor you use to write letters. You can easily add photos and other style elements to your pages after learning a few basics with onscreen tutorials. Adobe GoLive and Macromedia Dreamweaver are programs that are available for both Mac and Windows systems. FrontPage is probably one of the simplest software programs for beginners, but is only available in Windows formatting at this time.

### Fact

Programs such as GoLive and Dreamweaver allow you to use powerful tools to design, but they show you how to keep your Web site simple if you're not ready yet to dig in deeper and use all the bells and whistles available.

Two important pros to building a Web site from scratch are design control and cost. The software is an expense but a storage space (hosting) might only cost you $6 to $8 per month, versus $100-plus to belong to a predesigned network. Your design will be unique, with no chance that agents around town will have the same preformatted look. Weigh the options to decide which route works best in terms of time management and expense.

Realtor.com (*www.realtor.com*) is the public Web site for the National Association of Realtors®. It is linked to most major MLS systems around the United States, displays all of their listings, and gives contact information for agents. When a listing sells or is updated in any way, Realtor.com reflects the changes. Agents and real estate firms can purchase larger Web sites within the Realtor.com network.

## Attracting Buyers and Sellers to Your Web Site

Once you have a Web site, how will people find it? You'll receive all kinds of e-mail from companies that offer to get your domain listed and ranked near the top in popular search engines like Google and Yahoo! They charge a hefty fee. Don't bother clicking the links they send you because there is nothing they can do for you that you cannot do for yourself.

### E Alert

People who use the Internet want action—now. If you don't respond to them right away they'll likely move on to someone who will. Check your e-mail as often as possible and respond to queries immediately, even if it's with a note that introduces yourself and says you'll send more information later that day.

One of the first things you should be aware of when you enter the Web is the phrase "search engine optimization," called SEO for short. It refers to the steps you take to get search engines to recognize your site and give it the highest ranking possible.

One way that is accomplished is with the use of meta tags. The term *meta* itself means "about." For Web pages, it refers to extra bits of information you supply the search engines to tell them about your page. Your software program's tutorial explains meta. Predesigned Web sites usually offer them as blanks for you to fill in.

## Meta Titles

Every Web page should have a meta title that describes the page content. This is not the title that people see within the text on your page; it's a title that's placed in the meta tag area of your document. You should only use letters and hyphens in your title, not special characters such as & and +. It's not always possible, but try to write your title to include words that you know people are searching for such as:

> Florida Condominiums for Sale—Beachfront Property For Sale
> Homes for Sale in Nºrth Carolina—Near Asheville and Blue Ridge Mountains
> Homes for Sale in Wyoming—Real Estate in Wyoming

Use terms that work for your area. Pretend you are a consumer looking for real estate and search for current listings in your area to see which local Web sites are ranked highest and how they use titles. The meta title is visible at the very top of individual Web pages.

### Question

**How will I know what terms people are searching for?**
There are several Web sites that allow you to see how many times a word has recently been searched on its system. You'll find Overture's word tool at *http://inventory.overture.com/d/searchinventory/suggestion.*

Predesigned Web sites sometimes do not allow you as much flexibility with title tags and page content, but most do offer at least a basic way to optimize your site for search engines. Your meta title is one of the most important parts of your page, so put some thought into its wording.

### Description Meta Tags

A meta description is a short paragraph that tells people what they can expect to see on the page. It is sometimes displayed when a search engine lists that page. Write descriptions to repeat the important words you used in your title and try not to repeat the same phrase over and over again. The computer that reads your meta tags will put you at the bottom of the list if you are too redundant.

### Meta Keywords

Meta keywords are words that you place in a specific field for search engines to browse. They should be words that describe the document. Each phrase is separated by a comma, as in the following example:

> real estate new york, homes for sale, new york homes, buffalo real estate

Do not repeat the same word more than five times or the search engine's automated information gatherer (called a robot) might think you are trying to "spam" it (trick it into thinking you have content on the page that you truly don't have).

### Keywords in Text

The term *keywords* is used again to describe words you use within the text of your document; the text that is actually visible when someone clicks on your page. Try to repeat the important words you chose for your title within the page itself to reinforce to search engines that the information you promise is really there. Use the words in the first paragraph of the document if possible and repeat them again later.

### Links to and from Other Web Sites

Link popularity helps your search engine placement. That means your ranking can go up if other Web sites add links to yours. Getting links is sometimes difficult for real estate agents, but you can try to get links from:

- Your local Chamber of Commerce or visitor's center
- Organizations you are a member of
- Web sites of the people you do business with: home inspectors, surveyors, etc.
- Your friends and family's Web sites
- The newspapers and other advertising companies you use

Offer to trade links with other area businesspeople. It will help you both rank higher in the search engines. Search engine optimization is an ever-changing topic. There are hundreds of Web sites devoted to teaching you the best methods to use to promote your domain. The majority of these Web sites charge you a fee, but you can get a feel for what they are selling and what they offer by checking a few such as *www.submitexpress.com* and *http://website-submission.com* or by typing "search engine optimization" into your search engine and scrolling through the results.

**Essential**

Being sure that your Web site is found on all the search engines is a start, but there are other ways to direct people to your Web site. Be sure your URL is listed on all your marketing materials including your business card, your advertising, your mailers, and your property flyers.

## *Virtual Tours*

The Internet is a visual marketplace, one where long paragraphs of text often remain unread but where photographs create attention and keep people exploring your Web site. Virtual tours take photographs a step further. They offer consumers an online walk-through of properties. If consumers like what they see in photos they'll be more likely to contact you to see the property in person.

### Fisheye Lenses

Most virtual tours are photographed using one of two methods. The first method uses a fisheye camera lens—a large lens that photographs a 180-degree view of what's in front of the lens and to the top, bottom, and sides of the camera. The view stretches much farther to each side of the camera than a wide-angle lens.

The photographer uses the fisheye lens to take one picture, then turns the camera around 180 degrees from the first position and shoots again. The images are uploaded to a computer where special software combines the photographs into one 360-degree picture (often called a panorama), which is placed on the Internet as a virtual tour.

The image in panorama moves as readers click on it with their computer mouse. It offers the same view you would see if you were standing in an area and turned your body in a full circle to view your surroundings from all angles.

Fisheye lenses can be expensive and they are not available for every camera. The manufacturer of this technology is iPix, which you'll find at *www.ipix.com*. The materials on their Web site can help you determine if the system is the best choice for your needs.

**Fact**

There are many individuals who will create iPix photos for you, for a fee. Your local MLS might have contact information for these individuals.

### Standard Lens Virtual Tours

Another type of virtual tour software lets you use any digital camera, equipped with any lens, to take photos for your virtual tours. The photographer takes a picture, then turns the lens slightly, taking another. The left portion of the second photo overlaps a portion of the first. The photographer continues to turn in a circle, taking more photos that overlap each other on one side.

The photographs are uploaded to a computer where special software analyzes them, detecting the overlapped areas on the edges of photographs. It automatically merges the photographs, matches up edges, and stitches them together to create a panorama. The panorama is placed on the Internet to become a virtual tour.

The end result of this method is a panorama that takes you around the photographed area, but, because it was not created with a fisheye lens, it doesn't include the uppermost or lower areas of the view. That's a plus to some people who tend to get a queasy feeling when viewing rounded, moving photos online—they compare the feeling to carsickness.

### Other Visuals

Some preformatted Web sites offer agents a slide-show view. It doesn't use panoramic photos, but it allows you to place a series of pictures online. The slide show starts automatically when a viewer clicks a button on the screen, moving one by one through the photographs that you have provided.

Some agents also use digital video and audio to promote their listings. Video with sound can be a powerful advertising tool. Think of a rushing stream, the sound of a waterfall, or the sound of birds singing from a private, wooded estate. Video and audio are just two more tools you can use to promote your listings on the World Wide Web.

## *Internet Data Exchange*

Placing all your listings on the Internet is one way to give them exposure, but what if you do not have any listings? You want to receive e-mails and phone calls requesting your assistance, but if you have nothing to sell but your services, you will get very little response.

In the year 2000 the National Association of Realtors® issued a ruling that allows their agents to advertise each other's listings on their Web sites. Originally called *broker reciprocity*, this system is now known as *Internet data exchange*, or IDX.

Many MLS services around the country now allow you to share all of their data on your Web site. This gives you the ability to link to the entire MLS while keeping people within your Web site, which means that the calls and e-mails can come to you.

You will be required to give credit to the agent or company who actually has the listing, but their information will be less prominent as it shows up within your personal site. Check with your MLS provider to see if they have a simple way of linking to your site. If they do not there are several IDX services that can help you.

As the Internet continues to change, the rules set out by your state division of real estate or your local Board of Realtors® will change as well. Be sure to stay informed as the evolution of IDX and other services available to agents continues.

Chapter 17

# If You Want to Specialize

**There are many** ways you can turn your real estate experience into a career that specializes in one aspect of the business. Your specialization can deal with the way you work with clients or with the types of things you sell or manage. Take some time to find and talk to the people who already specialize, to help determine if one of the available career paths is right for you.

## *Exclusive Buyer Agencies*

Some firms work only with real estate buyers, signing buyer agency contracts to make them legal buyer representatives. They focus purely on buyer needs and do not take listings at all because they feel that representing any seller creates a conflict with the work they do to make sure they are loyal to the needs of their buyers.

If you choose to work for an exclusive buyer agency you'll never represent a seller during a transaction. Working for only the buyer eliminates a great deal of the stress that occurs when you are responsible for looking after the interests of the seller too. You'll be free to reveal nearly any information to your buyer that will result in a better deal on the property.

Exclusive buyer's agents are nearly always compensated from the commission a seller pays at closing, but the contracts they sign with buyers usually stipulate that buyers will pay the commission if the agency cannot collect from a seller. That's not substantially different from the contracts used by buyer's agents at a traditional firm, which work with both buyers and sellers. Working in the buyer's best interest, and knowing that they are receiving compensation from the buyer, an agent may solicit homes that are not on the market or show their buyer property being offered by a for sale by owner.

Being an exclusive buyer's agent means that when your buyers become sellers, they will need to work with another agent. You will usually have fewer upfront costs than a listing agent (fewer marketing dollars to be spent), but you will need to be available to show property on an ongoing basis.

## Fact

Most exclusive buyer agency firms are located in areas with a very active real estate market. Firms in smaller markets sometimes feel they need the income from both buyer and seller clients to make a living.

The National Association of Exclusive Buyer Agents (NAEBA) is one of the educational organizations that firms can affiliate with to promote their buyer agency business. The NAEBA offers an educational Web site for buyers at *www.naeba.org* and a site for prospective and current agent members at *www.naeba.info*. The organization has an annual convention and offers agents the benefits of shared expertise among its members. The NAEBA awards the Certified Exclusive Buyer Agent designation (CEBA) for agent studies. All NAEBA members work only as exclusive buyer's agents for firms that deal exclusively with buyers.

REBAC, the Real Estate Buyer's Agent Council, is an organization that's affiliated with the National Association of Realtors®. It also offers its members a national convention and educational opportunities through the Accredited Buyer Representative designation (ABR). A manager's version of the designation is also available.

Many agents who hold the ABR designation work for firms that only contract with buyers, but most ABR agents work for traditional firms that represent both buyers and sellers. Read about more educational designations in Chapter 2.

## *Working in a Development*

Does your town have one or more large developments where new homes are being built? The sales efforts for new homes in developments might be handled by the developer's staff agents or by a single real estate firm.

Working in a development is a great choice for agents who like to specialize. Homes are often somewhat similar, so it's easy to learn their features. Working in a development also cuts down your driving time and fuel expense and you can learn a great deal about home construction if your duties include selling homes that aren't yet built.

E Alert

Some sales-related jobs in a real estate development do not require that you have a real estate license. Talk to several developers and real estate firms to become familiar with the types of opportunities available in your area.

A firm that specializes in a development also has a good chance of acquiring its resale listings when the houses are put on the market by their original owner. This is because owners often assume that the agency knows the area best and works with a large number of potential buyers.

## *Specializing in Land Sales*

Looking at licensed real estate agents as a group, you won't find a high percentage of them who handle only land sales, but some agents prefer to work with land whenever they have the opportunity. You can dress casually and you'll spend a lot of time outdoors previewing and showing property. Commissions are another plus. In some areas, agencies charge a higher fee to market and sell land than they do to sell homes.

If you sell land, you'll also learn to read a survey and find boundary lines. If you work with larger tracts of land, you will become accustomed to topographical maps, which have distinctive circular rings drawn on them to show a site's changing elevations. You might use a global positioning system (GPS) receiver, which relies on satellite tracking to tell you exactly where you are on Earth.

Selling land helps you become familiar with your community's zoning regulations and other related laws. Can your buyer build what she wants on the land you found for her? It sometimes takes a bit of research on your part to find out. Not everyone enjoys working in land sales but it might be the perfect specialization for you if you love to be outdoors.

### Fact

Agents interested in land sales can obtain the Accredited Land Consultant (ALC) designation, available by belonging to and taking instructional classes from the Realtors' Land Institute.

If there are strict governmental regulations for land development, due to environmentally sensitive lands or other factors, specializing in land sales can give you an edge over other agents who have less knowledge of the intricacies tied to development.

## Condominiums and Time-Shares

Condominiums are apartment-like homes located in multifamily buildings. The duties involved with selling condos depend a lot on where you work. If you're located in a large city, you'll find that condos are listed in the MLS and most firms take an active part in selling them. Firms that own one or more large condo complexes might handle all or many sales in-house, hiring agents like you to do the job for them.

Time-share sales began in Europe when property prices became so high that vacation homebuyers could no longer afford to buy a residence strictly for their own use.

Although time-share sales aren't widespread, if you live at a tourist destination, you might have a large time-share complex right next door, where you can work for the owner selling new and resale time-shares at that site or other sites within the same company.

**Question**

**What's the difference between a condo and a townhouse?**
The owner of a townhouse also owns the land beneath the structure. The owner of a condo owns only the portions of the structure within the unit's walls, not the land or common areas such as shared stairs and hallways.

There are also real estate firms that specialize in time-share resales, taking listings for owners just as other firms list homes. They list time-shares in many locations, not necessarily within their town or state. Don't accept a position at a time-share resale firm without investigating the firm thoroughly. While there are some excellent agencies out there, there are unfortunately many others that do not abide by real estate laws and that treat clients in an unethical manner.

## Commercial Real Estate Sales

Commercial properties include buildings and businesses that people purchase as an investment. Investors can rent their commercial properties to tenants who seek a place to house offices and other businesses, or they can use the properties to operate the businesses themselves.

Most agents who sell strictly commercial properties began their careers as residential sales agents, then switched to a commercial specialization after they acquired a good understanding of the skills required to do that job effectively. In small towns or other areas where commercial opportunities aren't as plentiful, many agents sell both residential and commercial real estate, rather than specializing in one or the other.

Commercial real estate agents must be able to analyze the potential income returns an investor can expect from a commercial property. They must be aware of zoning issues and local laws that affect real estate and business owners. Commercial agents are privy to details about their clients' finances, so they must be people who can be trusted with confidential information. They aren't expected to be tax professionals, but they must have a good understanding of tax laws and how those laws impact their clients.

Finding a mentor who is successful in commercial real estate (and who wants to pass on her knowledge) can be an important training tool. You can learn the ins and outs of commercial real estate on your own, but it is so much easier and less time consuming if you have someone you know you can call when you have a question.

Most commercial agents do not hold the Certified Commercial Investment Member (CCIM) designation, but it is an excellent education program that everyone who is serious about commercial real estate should explore. The CCIM organization offers its members more than educational opportunities. It's a network of professionals who interact with and promote one another's businesses. The designation is not easy to obtain, but you'll learn what you need to know about commercial real estate and make important contacts during the process.

## Property Management

One of the most popular specialties in real estate is property management. Some agents do not even help clients buy or sell—they only manage properties. Some do a combination of both, managing properties that they have sold to an investor. Because more than 30 percent of the sales in recent years are not primary properties but rentals or second homes, the role of a property manager has become increasingly important.

Fast-paced and filled with stressful situations, property management is definitely a "love it or hate it" career. Managing properties is most suitable for a real estate agent who is organized enough to juggle many duties at once and who interacts easily with a wide variety of personalities.

You'll work with property owners who pay you to manage their real estate. You'll work with their tenants, and you'll work closely with repair people, landscapers, service personnel, and anyone else whose skills are needed to keep the property in good condition.

**Fact**

According to the National Association of Realtors®, 23 percent of the homes purchased in 2004 were for investment and an additional 13 percent were purchased as vacation homes. This is a great opportunity for an agent who wants to specialize in property management.

### Why Choose Property Management?

Real estate sales can create an unpredictable income stream and, for some people, that makes for an uncomfortable situation. They like the idea of making more money based on their efforts but they also like the idea of knowing how much to budget for each month.

Generally, property managers have a more predictable income, but it is still based on performance. If you manage twenty homes with an average fee of $75 per month per home, you will have a predictable gross income of $1,500 per month. If you manage fifty homes at $75 per month, your income increases to $3,750 per month. Of course, a predictable income comes with a more rigid schedule than the flexible income and flexible schedule of the sales agent. As a property manager, you will need to be available at the first of the month to collect rents. You will need to be available when there is a vacancy in order to show the properties, and you will need to be available to handle the details if there is a maintenance problem. You will still have moderate flexibility within these guidelines, so if a predictable income appeals to you, this may be your specialty.

### Duties of a Property Manager

The main functions of a property manager are to find and qualify tenants, collect rents, and ensure that maintenance is performed and that nonpaying tenants are removed through the eviction process or by other means. Checking on vacant properties to be sure there has been no vandalism, broken pipes, or other damage, preparing the properties for rent, and accounting for money are also part of the duties of a property manager.

Although there are tenant advocates who work for the tenant, a property manager generally works for the owner of the property. No matter how wonderful the tenant is, your fiduciary duty as property manager is owed to the owner. Property managers are a buffer between an owner and the owner's tenants. As a property manager, you collect rents and deal with people who can't pay or must pay late. You are the person tenants call when something breaks down and you are the one who in turn calls a repair person to schedule a time to fix the problem. You also verify that the job was done correctly.

### Essential

Some property managers are paid a salary and others earn a commission that is a percentage of the rents collected. The National Association of Realtors® reports that the average income for a property management specialist is more than the average income among sales agents.

More complaints are filed against property managers than real estate agents working in other specialties. In part, this is because managers work with so many different people, raising the odds that at least a portion of them will be unhappy. It's essential for managers to keep detailed records of transactions and to make sure they are covered by ample errors and omissions insurance.

## Handling Money

The rental funds a property manager collects must be placed in a trust account, which is not intermingled with other money. If you work in a large property management firm you might not be directly responsible for handling incoming rents and outgoing payments to service people and property owners. However, you should understand the laws that govern how those funds are handled, so that you can step into that position if required and so you will recognize if someone appears to be handling funds improperly.

### Alert

More real estate agents lose their licenses after mishandling trust funds than for any other reason. Handle trust funds and keep records exactly as the law requires, and you shouldn't have any problems.

Your state real estate laws dictate how trust funds must be handled. Money held in trust is money that someone has given to you but belongs to someone else. In property management the rents belong to your clients (the property owners), even though you eventually use a portion of them to pay yourself and other service personnel.

## Repair and Maintenance Issues

As the property manager, start by ensuring that the home you are going to rent out is in its best possible condition. It may be wise to get an inspection from a licensed home inspector and have all issues handled before starting the process. Ask the home inspector to point out cosmetic items as well as other maintenance issues, such as torn or missing screens. Start with having the owner take care of every defect the home inspector discovers. If the owner is not willing or not able to take care of any defect, the house may still work well as a rental as long as you, the owner, and any prospective tenant note that defect.

### Fact

Sometimes replacing a cracked floor tile means replacing an entire floor. As long as the crack does not appear to be of the type that will get worse, disclosing this without fixing it can be sufficient.

Photographing the house is a great way to get a detailed record of its condition. If you are using a digital camera, be sure to have the photographs printed so that no one can accuse you of using a program like Photoshop to doctor the pictures later on. Give a set to the tenant and have them sign the back of each photo as approval of the condition and place that set in the file. When the tenant moves out you can easily determine if there was any damage by taking "after" pictures and comparing them. Once again, due to the nature of digital photos, it is best to take the after pictures and print them in the company of the tenant. Taking photos of a house for rental purposes is different from taking photos for enjoyment. You will need to take photographs of the following:

- Each and every wall of each and every room
- The floors of every room
- The ceilings of every room
- The doors
- The interior of the tubs/showers
- The appliances, including the interiors of the oven and refrigerator
- The exterior and interior of the fireplace or woodstove
- The garage
- Any other feature that is particular to the house

The tenant will also need to fill out a move-in statement. They will make note of anything in the house that needed attention before they moved in. Most states have a form that can be used with check boxes to keep the tenant from forgetting anything. This form needs to be signed by the tenant and by you and kept in your file.

Once a tenant moves into the house, if they pay the rent on time and you don't get any complaints from the neighbors, chances are you will not set foot in the house during their tenancy. This can be good and bad. Some tenants won't tell you when something is wrong with the house. They are worried that you will raise the rent or ask them to move if there is a maintenance issue.

The danger of this lack of communication is evident in the following example. Imagine that a couple moved into a house and paid rent faithfully for many years. During that time there was a leak in the bathroom, which they did not report to the landlord. When they moved out they left the property in excellent condition and at first glance it appeared that they would receive their security deposit back.

**Essential**

Keep a reserve of cash to take care of the little things that may crop up. If you have a heater go out in the middle of winter and the owner lives in another community, you want to be able to get the heat on, even if you can't reach the owner for payment right away.

As the landlord went through the property for his final walk-through, he heard the sound of water dripping. When he went to check it, he discovered that the floor of the bathroom was soft. Upon closer inspection he could see that a leak had been going on for a long time, and that, as a result, the tub was ready to fall through the floor! If the tenant had called when the leak first started, the repair would have been simple. Now it will be an expensive repair and the potential for mold problems exists as well.

What could have been done to prevent this? As a property manager, it is your duty to inspect the properties you manage on a regular basis, even if there is no problem with the tenant. This inspection can occur once every few months, or even once a year, depending on the age of the house and whether or not the tenant calls you about repairs or other issues with the house. Some tenants will call for every little detail that they think needs to be repaired. They may even call for things that are their responsibility such as a burned-out light bulb. As much of a time waster as these tenants appear to be, they may actually be better tenants than the ones who keep quiet—at least you know that the house is being taken care of.

## Vacation Rentals

Having a vacation rental department is like running a hotel except that your rooms are not in one building but all over town. By creating a system, you will have an easier time of running your "hotel." For example, if every property has the same white bedding, it can all be washed together and redistributed back to the different locations.

Vacations are all about enjoying time off. When people choose a vacation rental over a conventional hotel, they are looking for all the comforts of home, away from home. If you've ever vacationed in accommodations that didn't meet your expectations, you understand the importance of having everything you need. You also know how not having those conveniences can change your vacation experience for the worse.

In addition to meeting a guest's expectations, anticipating their needs and having the basic necessities can help protect the property. For instance, putting a corkscrew in the kitchen drawer will prevent the guest's need to improvise by using a knife instead, thereby avoiding injury to the knife and the guest.

Many vacation rental companies require certain items in all of their rentals. (See Appendix A for a list of suggested items in a vacation rental.) You will also discover certain things that work well regionally, such as sleds in mountain communities or water toys at the beach.

## Commercial Rentals

As a rental manager for commercial properties, chances are you will have tenants for a longer period of time. Most commercial leases are a minimum of five years and they can have options that last twenty years or more. In general, tenants are required to do their own improvements and they take care of their own interior repairs. Often exterior repairs are paid for by the tenants on a prorated by-square-footage basis. This may sound like the easiest type of property management, but it does have its downside.

Due to the less than hands-on nature of running commercial property, many owners take on the responsibility of managing the property themselves, leaving fewer opportunities to manage commercial property. When there is a vacancy it can take months or even years to fill. Advertising may have to be done nationally to find the right tenant for the property. The costs associated with a vacancy can create tension between the owner and the property manager and it can affect the property manager's income stream as well.

## *Special Training*

The National Association of Residential Property Managers (NARPM) holds an annual convention for its members and gives them the opportunity to take one- and two-day property management classes. Classes cover issues such as operations, maintenance, marketing your listings, risk management, tenancy, and other important topics, and they allow individuals to obtain special designations.

### Fact

Every major organization that offers special designations for its members also has a code of ethics that members are expected to follow. Your membership can be revoked if you violate an ethics code.

The organization offers three special designations. Designations are awarded in ascending order, as the agent takes classes and builds experience. Over and above the requirements for a real estate license, many states require additional education in order to engage in property management services.

1. Residential Management Professional (RMP)
2. Master Property Manager (MPM)
3. Certified Residential Property Manager (CRPM)

Property managers can often acquire training on a local level from the same licensing schools that conduct continuing-education classes for agents. Your firm might also provide in-house training to help teach you the business of property management. Some states also require additional licensing to become a property manager, so check your state's division of real estate to see what your state requires.

Chapter 18

# Client Record Keeping

**You have learned** that in order to keep your business thriving, keeping in touch is the key. To do this, you need a record-keeping system that doesn't leave everything to chance, or to your memory. When you start out, you may remember whom to call and when to call them, but as your business grows, so does the possibility of forgetting someone or something important. Learn to use record-keeping and organization tools when your business is small and your business will run more smoothly as it expands.

## *The Basics*

Keeping records of your clients and your appointments can be done in a number of ways. The method you use is less important than the fact that you have a method. Find what works best for you and record information consistently. There are two main options for keeping track of your clients, each with its own set of positive and negative features: electronic record keeping and paper record keeping.

### Electronic

Many agents work with a personal digital assistant, or PDA. This piece of equipment is actually a hand-held computer. It keeps everything at your fingertips: your contact list, their information, your calendar and any appointments you may have, as well as your to-do list. The advanced PDA also doubles as a cellular phone and digital camera. A PDA also interfaces with your computer. This means that all the information on the PDA can be downloaded and stored on your computer. If you do use a PDA, it is best to back it up to your main computer at least once a day.

There are many different PDAs on the market and some can even display your MLS information. Check with your local association to see what brands have the technology to work in conjunction with your MLS. There are many popular brands and some less-known PDAs. The names you will hear most often are Palm Pilot, Pocket PC, BlackBerry, and Psion. Spend some time researching each one and find the PDA that has features you find easy to use. If it is too complicated for you, you will probably not use it often.

### Paper

If the idea of learning how to use a PDA intimidates you, or if you are not ready to spend the money on one, it is still important to keep track of everything. You can do this with a calendar, a notepad, and an address book. The best type of paper format is a daily planner, where all these tools are together in one book.

It is best to keep the planner with you at all times. This will allow you to retrieve phone numbers while you are out, add appointments to your calendar, and add notes to your to-do list.

**E Alert**

You should only have one calendar. All your appointments, whether personal or business, should be in the same place. You do not want to accidentally have a listing presentation and a doctor's appointment at the same time!

Because you will be carrying it with you all the time, be sure your planner is of a size and type that is convenient for you. Do you need an oversized planner so that you remember to carry it or a small planner that will fit into a briefcase or purse? Decide what will work for you and use it faithfully. Every office supply store carries a number of different styles.

You can also check into the most popular brands such as Day-Timer, Day Runner, Franklin Planner, and Tax Reduction Institute Diary. Many of these have software programs that work just like the written version. Once you get used to the system, you can easily convert to an electronic system later. Of course, you will have to add everything from the written format into the electronic version but, if you are organized, this should not be too time consuming.

### Combination Electronic and Paper

Many agents use a combination of electronic and paper organizers to keep track of their clients. They will have all their client and customer contact information on their main computer, and keep the phone numbers stored in their cell phone as well. These agents may carry an appointment book or calendar with them, but they will leave the to-do list in an electronic form on their office computer or on a yellow pad at their desk where they can cross off items as they complete them. Having your to-do list in one place, rather than on hundreds of sticky notes, will usually keep you from missing an important item.

**Essential**

Any record-keeping system or combination of systems can be used. The secret is to use the system you choose consistently. No system works if you don't use it!

## *Don't Lose Track of New Prospects*

New prospects often start by shopping for an agent. They may have been referred to one or two agents and they may have found some through advertising or the Internet. These prospects have not yet developed loyalty to a single agent. The quality of your contact with them will help develop their loyalty toward you.

Placing these prospects on your calendar for a follow-up every few days can keep you in the forefront of their minds. Ask them what their needs are. If they are planning to sell, offer them a market analysis, even if they are not going to be ready for a period of time. If they are planning to purchase, find out what their criteria are and keep a look out for suitable properties. You should notify them anytime something comes on the market that fits their needs. You should also be in touch even if there isn't anything available for them yet. Let them know about "almost" properties such as a home in their budget that may be a bit smaller than they had hoped to find.

**E Alert**

Although e-mail has become more prevalent, there are still many people who do not use it or who do not use it consistently. Don't assume your clients and customers use e-mail regularly. Ask them what method of communication they prefer and use that method when sending them regular updates.

If your MLS system allows for it, you can set it up so that your prospects receive regular updates as new properties become available. If this service is not available through your MLS, you can still perform the function manually by inputting their criteria on a regular basis and e-mailing the results. Follow up with a phone call, because not everyone checks e-mail diligently. Your e-mail may also look like spam to some spam filters and could end up as junk mail instead of being sent to your client's in-box. You can use the call to be sure the client received the e-mail. If you do use the automatic e-mail system, be sure that it also sends you the same updates. This way if they call you about a certain property you will have the information at hand.

## Keeping in Touch with Your Clients

Current and past clients and customers are just as important as new prospects. These are people who are already loyal to you. It is your job to keep them loyal, not only for the potential of future business with them but because your current and past clients and customers are your greatest source of referrals. Maintain records of all of your dealings with clients and set up reminders on your computer or in your address book to ensure that you are keeping them updated and that you are maintaining your professional relationship with them.

### Current Sellers

Current clients who are sellers like to know what is going on with their home and with the market. Make it a habit to call them on a regular basis, even if you don't have an offer. Let them know about your most recent marketing efforts, tell them the news of a neighbor's sale and why you think it happened before theirs (the neighbor was asking less, they had a bigger yard, etc.).

**Essential**

Cut out or copy all of your print advertising and mail it to your selling clients on a weekly or bimonthly basis. Send them copies of the flyer and any other marketing material, such as just-listed postcards. This will show them that you are earning your fee.

In the case of a client, no news is bad news. Make sure clients know what you are doing and give them feedback from other people who saw their house, along with any other information. Even if you have no news, call them and tell them you have no news! They are waiting on pins and needles for any information you may give them. By providing them exceptional service they will be confident referring you to their friends and family. Be sure to let them know that your profession is a referral-based profession. It is okay to ask them for referrals.

Some agents set up a specific time each week to give their client an update. When you first sign a listing contract, you may want to ask which day is best and arrange to call them on that day. If you do not set up weekly updates, the client may expect daily updates, even if they don't tell you that. By predetermining when you will be calling each week, they will know what to expect. In a fast-paced market, you may need to set up a daily update. In a slow market, it may be once every two weeks.

### Current Buyers

Current clients or customers who are buyers also like to know what is going on with the market. They like to hear if anything has come on the market that they may be interested in, but they also like to know if nothing has come on the market.

If the buyer has already purchased and is waiting for a close, you will want to be in touch with her on a regular basis. If it is a quick close, you may need to call the buyer with an update every day. In a longer transaction, you may call every few days or once a week. Once you receive an accepted offer, you will want to set up the times that you will be calling. Let your client know if the title search has been done, what papers need to be signed and when, the time of the home inspection, and any other pertinent information. If nothing is happening or if everything is running smoothly, let them know that too. Often, agents will only bother their clients with problems—so a smooth transaction can go unrewarded.

**Fact**

Buyers who follow the market through the Internet feel more confident in you if you call to tell them about something before they find it themselves online. By keeping clients up to date on opportunities, you prove that you are looking out for their best interest and show them what they can expect if they refer you to friends and family.

### Past Clients

Within a year of selling their home, many people will tell you they had a great experience, liked their agent, thought he did a good job, and would be happy to refer him—but most of them can't remember their agent's name! Staying in touch with your past clients will keep this from happening to you. The more personalized your contact is, the better. In the time you set aside to prospect, call past clients first. These are people who are already pleased with you. They will be happy to hear from you, especially because real estate agents have the reputation for vanishing after the close of a deal, after they get paid.

**Essential**

When contacting past clients, ask them if there is anything they need. Let them know about a tidbit of information they may find helpful (such as garbage day in your neighborhood is being changed from Wednesday to Thursday, starting the first of the year).

The more clients you have, the harder it will be to make every contact personalized on a regular basis, but you can use other methods to stay in touch as well. Newsletters or other general information will help keep you in the forefront of their minds. Be sure that what you send is something helpful and is something they can use. You will still want to call people on a regular basis. Perhaps instead of once a month you will call once a quarter.

## *Remembering Special Events*

Placing special events on a calendar will help you to remember them. You won't have a problem with obvious events like national holidays, but put them on the calendar anyway if you plan to acknowledge your clients at the time. You may not remember your client's birthday or house anniversary without placing that information on a calendar. Be sure to place the event on your calendar a few days in advance of the actual date to give you time to mail a card or pick up a small, personalized gift that you could possibly deliver. It's a great way to see your clients face to face, find out if they need anything, and ask for referrals.

## *Setting Up Your To-Do List*

Your to-do list is comprised of many items, from keeping in touch with people to the steps it takes to handle a transaction. As you complete the items on your to-do list, cross them out. Spend time every day working on the list. There are things that will stay on the list as you wait for other people to perform (call the lender for an update, leave a message) and there are things that can be crossed off immediately. Your to-do list should be prioritized so that you take care of the most important matters first.

Some agents keep their daily to-do list on their calendar, with long-range to-do lists on a yellow pad or in their computer. You may also want two or three different to-do lists, one long range, one short range, and one daily list. Be sure to keep them all in the same place, perhaps on different pages of the same yellow pad. Sometimes a lower-priority item can move to a high priority if it is not taken care of promptly.

## *Agent Software Programs*

Agent software programs, sometimes called contact management programs, organize your clients so that you can more easily determine whom to call and when. Researching which program will work best for you is critical, because contact management programs, like other organization products, are not worth anything if you don't use them.

### Question

**How can I figure out what program to choose?**

Check with other agents in your office to find out what program they like, or take a class offered by one of the program's salespeople. Some CMPs are Top Producer (designed for real estate agents), Profit for Outlook, Act!, and GoldMine. Your MLS may have a contact management program available for its members but be sure it can move with you if you change offices.

Shop for a software package that is easy for you to use and that has the capability to aid you with the things you want to accomplish. With a good software program, you will be able to sort your database of clients in a number of ways. The most common sorting methods are alphabetical by name, by address, by type of client, by clients' needs, and by date of contact. There are many software programs, some complex and some simple. Some were designed especially for real estate agents and some are for anyone in sales. Some are only databases and cannot be searched in various ways. Be sure the program you are looking at has a multiple search function, and learn what you can about each program before purchasing one.

Once you have a contact management program to help you get organized, input all of your contacts in the program, including their name, address, phone numbers, e-mail addresses, and the type of contact they are. This way, you can not only sort contacts by name and date of input, but also by what type of contact they are.

Contact types can include:

- Current buyers
- Current sellers
- Past buyers
- Past sellers
- Future buyers
- Future sellers
- Family
- Friends
- Acquaintances
- Neighbors
- Previous work colleagues
- Owners or employees of the businesses you frequent
- Schoolmates
- Church, temple, or other religious organization
- PTA
- Service clubs and organizations
- Gym or athletic pursuits (such as a bowling league or golf club)
- Veterans you served with
- Title companies
- Escrow companies
- Closing attorneys
- Other attorneys
- Lenders
- Home inspectors
- Local agents
- Out-of-town agents
- Contractors/repair services/trades people

You should enter all of the support people you need, such as title companies, lenders, and home inspectors. By putting in real estate agents from other communities (to whom you can send referrals and from whom you can receive referrals) and local agents (whom you may contact when marketing a property), you will be able to find everyone necessary to the functioning of your business with a few keystrokes on the computer.

Be sure the contact management program you purchase allows you to set up an alert schedule that will remind you of important dates, calls, or contacts you need to make. This feature can keep you from missing deadlines and help maintain your birthday, house anniversary, and special occasion card schedule.

## *The Paper Alternative*

If you do not have a computer or access to one where you can store your personal contact list, you can create a temporary system using a card file. Create two cards for everyone in your sphere of influence. File one card alphabetically and the other by the date you need to contact them next. Although this does not allow you to sort by category, it will be a decent start until you are able to purchase your own computer.

Keeping track of all of your contacts is easy when you don't have too many contacts, and contact management software might seem like overkill when you are a new agent. Keep in mind though that having a system in place at the beginning of your career in real estate will make it easy to keep your contact list updated and organized as your business expands.

Chapter 19

# Opening Your Own Agency

**Being your own** boss may have been one factor that motivated you to become a real estate agent. Taking that motivation one step further may manifest itself in a desire to open your own office. The endeavor can be both frustrating and rewarding. You will have the ultimate word in any decision, but you will also have the ultimate liability. You cannot blame any failures on the broker, but you can take full credit for your successes.

## *Analyzing Your Motivations*

Agents seek to open their own offices for many reasons, but the primary incentive is autonomy. Is autonomy the reason you want to open your own office? Are you planning to open your own office because you don't think anyone can do it as well as you? Are you thinking about it because you have personality differences with other brokers and can't work for someone else? Do you have agents in your current office who drive you crazy? Do you think you give too much money to your current office and believe you can run a real estate business for less? All of these questions need to be answered before you make a decision.

## *Your Mission Statement*

A good business plan starts with a statement of what you want to accomplish by having your own office. This is called a mission statement. A mission statement tells people what you are all about. It is your vision. A mission statement is like a slogan but it is also a summary of your direction as a company. It is short, usually three or four sentences, and it sums up who you are, what you provide, and where you want to go. It is not a bragging statement such as, "I am the best agent in the business." It is a statement of who you are and what you offer.

Are you all about client service? Are you all about agent support? Your mission statement can be simple, such as, "To provide exceptional real estate service from a positive working environment by building client relationships that enhance the referral base of the business and create a long-lasting stream of repeat customers and clients."

### Essential

Check with your state division of real estate to see what the guidelines are. Some states require that all brokers who own their own office have a certain number of years of experience working under another broker. Some require a certain net worth or credit score. Be sure you qualify under the state guidelines before starting out on your own.

Once you have discovered your mission statement, you will want to expand upon it. That expansion will take the form of a business plan.

## Create a Business Plan

Knowing in what direction you want your business to move will mark the start of your business plan. Your business plan will also encompass all of the "nuts and bolts" of starting and operating the business, including the costs and the policies.

When starting a business, most people underestimate the associated costs. They are either inexperienced as to what costs to expect or they are naive as to how much those costs will be. The steps to creating a business plan are simple to read but often difficult to implement:

1. Create a vision statement
2. Create a budget
3. Create an image

Take your time. You want to be sure that your business plan is as detailed as possible. You may even want to consider purchasing a business plan software program. There are also other resources available to you, including the Service Corps of Retired Executives (SCORE), which is a resource partner with the U.S. Small Business Administration. SCORE is a nonprofit with more than 10,500 volunteers, who provide free and confidential small business advice. The volunteers are working/retired business owners, executives, and corporate leaders. You can find their Web site at *www.score.org*.

### Franchise vs. Independent

Deciding whether to be independent or part of a franchise will determine the direction your office takes. There are advantages and disadvantages to both. Your market place, as well as your business style, will be a factor in making the decision. Franchises offer many benefits, from national advertising to products, services, and training. They also have associated costs. As an agent in a franchise, you pay a percentage of your commission off the top with every transaction. The amount is generally 6 to 8 percent. As a franchise office, that cost may be determined differently. The franchiser may have a monthly base rate, which you will be required to pay even if there are no transactions that month. They may charge a base rate plus a percentage or it may be a straight percentage. Meet with the franchiser and determine what the true costs are for an office, and what services they provide for that price.

**E Alert**

You may or may not qualify to own a franchise. Franchisers require franchisees to meet certain guidelines to maintain their reputation. They expect a minimum number of transactions or a minimum gross commission income. They have criteria for competition between their franchisees and only allow a certain number of franchises per area.

Most franchises have special policies that you are expected to follow. Some of these are required and others are optional. As an example, RE/MAX franchises often charge their agents a flat desk rent fee rather than a percentage of every transaction. Keller Williams has a profit-sharing plan and every agent is an owner of the Keller Williams franchise. A franchise also offers referrals from other offices within their franchise, but you may have to meet certain guidelines in order to receive those referrals.

Independent offices do not have the costs of a franchise but they face the challenge of creating their own branding and establishing a reputation. Many independent offices charge an advertising fee to cover that cost—you may decide to do that as well. Though they don't usually garner national name recognition, good independent offices will gain regional recognition if they brand themselves well. They have the additional costs of creating an image, but they also have the freedom to create the exact image they desire. Independent offices can still receive referrals from other offices. These referrals are usually from other independents who belong to a referral network or who have agents with special designations such as GRI or CRB.

### Starting from Scratch or Buying an Existing Office

It is possible that an existing office is available to purchase in your area. The broker may be retiring or moving to another area. Purchasing an existing office can be a similar cost, or a bit less expensive, than starting your own office. Once you have determined what it will cost to start from scratch, compare that to the cost of purchasing an existing office. An existing office may have inventory, agents, a location, a database of past clients, and a good reputation upon which you can build. They may have an established image and a long-standing telephone number. All of these can add value to the start of your business. Of course, the existing office could also be old and tired or it could have a less than desirable reputation.

If you purchase an existing office, there are many ways to make the transition smooth. The original broker can send out announcement cards that you are continuing the tradition of excellence that she has established, so as to retain some of the old office's clients and help you gain new business. You will want to meet with the agents to see if they are willing to stay on at the agency. Are you also buying a rental department with its assets and its headaches? If the office you work in now is available to purchase, your familiarity with its business practice may make the transition easier.

## *Finding the Perfect Location*

Many offices depend on "walk-ins." These are potential clients and customers who walk in the door looking for an agent. Sometimes walk-ins are just curious and waste the agent's time, but much of the time they are serious. If your market depends on walk-ins, your location should support that. If not, you can expand to alternate locations that do not depend entirely on foot traffic. Either way, your location should have good exposure, good signage, good lighting, and parking. If you are planning to start small but hope to have a larger office later, see if the location has room for growth without moving to a completely new facility. See what types of other businesses are in that area. Are there lots of offices or is it a mix of retail and other types of businesses? A real estate office can often get lost in a sea of attorneys and accountants but can easily be found next to a popular lunch spot or mixed in with boutique retail stores.

## *Start-up Expenses*

There are many costs associated with opening an office. Not only will you need desks and a phone system, but you will need computers and other equipment as well. Your start-up expenses will also include your image. Are you planning to purchase secondhand desks or will everything match and look slick and modern? What name will you use? Do you have a logo?

### Essential

Researching the true hard costs for starting a business, and assuming that they will be higher, can keep you out of financial trouble. Once you have determined the costs you believe to be accurate, add 25 percent or more to that number to account for any unforeseen costs.

The primary reason most businesses fail is lack of planning. Believing that you can go forward and start a business without a plan, especially without a financial plan, is a sure ticket to disaster. To get an idea of what your expenses will be, make a list of all the expenditures necessary to open your office, including:

- A good location
- Tenant improvements and upgrades
- Creating an image, branding
- Business license
- Membership to the local Board of Realtors® and/or MLS
- Phone system
- Copier
- Fax machine
- Computer
- Necessary software
- Printer
- Scanner
- Digital camera
- Desks
- Chairs
- File cabinets
- Office supplies
- Forms
- Stationery
- Logo and image design

Spend some time scouting out possible locations and the costs of rents. Find out if there are any additional costs associated with renting an office space. Commercial rentals are usually priced on a per-square-footage basis. How much square footage will you need? You can determine your square footage needs by deciding how many agents you will have and how much space is needed for each desk (the number of agents you need is explained later in this chapter), how much space is needed for a conference room, storage for files, a place for a coffeepot and small refrigerator, as well as other spaces you feel are necessary.

Ask the landlord if there are additional costs, over and above the rent. Utilities are rarely included, so you will need to include these costs in your budget. Many rentals are priced at what is called "triple net," which means that you pay your rent as well as a prorated portion of all the expenses based on your square footage in relation to others in your commercial complex.

### E Alert

Some commercial rentals charge a percentage of your profits. If this is the case, the commercial landlord will need to see your financial records and they also have the opportunity to audit you. This is not a recommended scenario. It opens you up to liability for incorrect postings of profits and it gives someone access to your financial picture.

Once you have determined a location and the cost of it, you will also need to determine the costs of potential tenant improvements. Do you need to make the bathrooms handicap accessible in order to get a business license? Will you need partitions, a kitchenette, or other additions? Are items installed by a previous tenant taking up valuable space? Can they be removed? How about paint and carpet?

Find out what type of deposit is necessary to secure the rental as well as how much you will need to pay the day you move in. Be sure to have at least six months of expenses set aside, because you don't want to be evicted just because the market is slow for a few months.

Determine the costs of each of the other items that you need to open the office. Go to the office supply store and price out desks, chairs, and supplies. Check with your local printer for the costs of stationery. Contact a design or advertising firm to determine the cost of a corporate identity and logo treatment. Once you have a realistic handle on the costs of opening and running an office, it is time to decide how many agents you need to help you keep the office running. You won't know if you can afford the overhead until you know what your income will be.

## Recruiting Agents

How many agents do you need and how much do they need to produce? A stable of good, productive agents will allow you to pay the costs of running the office and (hopefully) generate a profit. There are many ways to recruit agents, but the two most popular ways are through the real estate school or by recruiting them away from other offices.

### Fact

One of the lesser-known methods of recruiting, but one that can be done successfully, is to recruit someone from another business. Offer to pay for their real estate school and ask them to commit to working with you for a period of time. By granting success to someone, you also receive great loyalty.

It is important to have a mix of people that will work well together but who have different styles. The different styles will allow people who chose your office, because of your image or location, to pick the type of agent that they can work best with from a variety of personality styles. You will also need to think about what you can offer them, from the commission split to the working environment.

Determine the number of agents you need by first determining your costs. If your costs are 100 percent of what you need and each agent can produce enough income to cover 20 percent of what you need, you will want to have five agents to break even and more to generate a profit.

Take the average sales price of a listing, the average commission from that property, and the average office split that the transaction will bring your office. Assuming that the average sales price is $200,000, the average commission for one side of the transaction is $6,000, and the office takes 40 percent of that, or $2,400. Your office will take in $2,400 in office earnings and you, as the agent, will earn $3,600. It is generally believed that the average real estate agent does eight transactions per year. You will have big producers who do more and smaller producers who do less. The average agent will generate $19,200 per year. If it costs you $75,000 per year to run the office, you will need just a little better than four agents to break even ($76,800) and more to make a profit.

You must also consider how to best train your agents. Many franchises offer postlicensing courses for their agents. If you belong to a franchise, having your agents take one of these classes (usually two weeks long) is a great idea. If you are an independent, you may need to create your own classes. There are also many personal trainers and seminar leaders who can help direct your agents. Be sure your agents have good training, because if they make a mistake, as the broker you are ultimately responsible.

## *Creative Advertising and Your Unique Image*

The process of creating a vision statement and a business plan provides clues to your image. You may have used words like service, professional, or locally owned. If you do not know how to develop an image, or you only have a vague idea of how you want it to look, take your vision statement and business plan to an image consultant or advertising agency and have that company develop the image for you. Your image will stay with you, so it is worth spending some time and money on making it just right.

## *Your Policies and Procedures Manual*

Your policies and procedures manual will be a fluid document. You must update and change it to adapt to situations as they arise. Start with the things you believe will be an issue in your office. How will floor time be handled? Is there a dress code? How are the phones answered? In what order are referrals given out? How are generic calls handled versus calls that originate because an individual agent paid extra to advertise for them? What happens to an agent's clients when the agent is not in the office? Every time a new conflict occurs, a policy must be written for it. The first version of your manual should include things you know can occur.

Your policies and procedures manual should be dated. When changes occur they should be noted as changes in a dated document, as well as revised in the main manual. Some examples of possible policies you may want to include in your manual are photo policies, such as requiring a uniform look for professional photos; clarifying rules, such as a marketing department that must approve all ads; or assigning duties, such as stating that a certain position is responsible for importing the listing information to the MLS computer. Other things to consider when writing your policies and procedures manual are:

- What are the penalties for noncompliance?
- Do you fire people for being rude?
- What is the commission structure you expect your agents to charge?
- How will commission splits be determined?

Even the obvious may need to be in the policies and procedures manual, things such as "agents must empty their own trash daily." Every agent should review your manual and sign a document stating so.

## Do You Want a Rental Department?

Depending on the size of your office, you may decide to include a rental department to service the investors in your marketplace. If you do, you can either handle the property management duties yourself, along with your management duties, or hire a property manager to work for you. Having more than one source of income is the reason many offices choose to add a rental department.

Only one person or team in your office should handle rentals. This gives you the ability to keep better control—remember that renting property is the part of the real estate profession with the highest liability. Your property manager should not handle sales. This will give your sales agents incentive to bring rental properties to the office for a small referral fee. They will know that when their client goes to sell their rental property, the rental manager won't end up becoming their listing agent. Remember that property management is a labor-intensive part of the real estate profession, so be sure you are ready for the commitment.

Having your own office can be the most exciting thing you will ever do in your real estate career. If you create a profitable company with a positive image and an excellent reputation, you may have an office that someone else will purchase when you are ready to retire or if you decide to try your hand at a new profession.

Chapter 20

# Skills for Success

**You have learned** that being a real estate agent is more than just putting up a sign or putting someone in your car for the afternoon and making the big money with no effort on your part. Being a real estate agent requires education that continues throughout your career. It is more than luck that gets properties to sell. Every sale requires proper marketing and good negotiation skills. To acquire a consistent stream of sellers and buyers, you must cultivate new relationships, maintain existing relationships, and ask for business.

## *Real-Life Lessons*

There are many things about being a real estate agent that you will learn as you pursue your career. These are lessons that can be learned not from school or a book, but from actually engaging in the business of real estate. Each person you encounter through your work will have different needs and different ways of conveying those needs. Some will express their needs directly and some will be more subtle. You will have some clients and customers who don't really understand what their needs are or don't know how to put them into words. When you encounter these clients, it is up to you to figure out what would best suit them in a property. You will learn how to understand people and your understanding will grow with each person you encounter.

You will learn much from your own real-life experiences with your clients and customers. You will also learn a lot from watching, and learning from, the real-life experiences of other agents and your broker. Spending time in the office, simply observing those working around you, will help you understand and gain a perspective on the experiences that all agents encounter.

### Alert

Some of the agents you observe will offer you a good example of how to be an agent and others will show you a poor example. A poor example is not always evident at first glance. An agent's financial success may blind you to the fact that their family life is in shambles or their health has deteriorated.

## Be a Good Observer

Understanding people is the most important skill a real estate agent can have. The more you watch others, the more you will understand them. Don't just observe your clients and customers, the agents in your office, and others in the real estate profession. Watch everyone you encounter and imagine what it must be like to be in his or her shoes. When someone is upset, try to see past his frustration and ask yourself why he is upset. When someone is happy or excited, look at the entire situation and determine what part of it makes her feel so good.

### Question

**Should I even watch people in the grocery store or at the beach?**
Yes. By seeing people in all situations and noting their behavior, you can gain a better understanding of what is important to them. You can transfer that understanding of human nature to encounters in your real estate career.

Observe your own actions and reactions as well. Did you push that client to act because you really need the money or because you really believe he will regret it if he doesn't buy that particular house? Being mindful of your own motivations will help you to be more insightful about the motivations of others. Did you skip your prospecting calls because you had too many rejections last time? It is easy to take each rejection personally, so instead of becoming upset, step back and imagine what the other person was thinking. Perhaps you caught them at a bad time, or maybe they have several friends in the real estate business all pushing to sell them a new house. Think about how you handled things, too. It is not always the other person who needs to make a change—sometimes it is you.

## What to Do with Criticism

You will encounter rejection and criticism throughout your career. Some of it will have nothing to do with you, but some of it will be on target. When this happens, try to separate yourself from the situation and see what the truth is in the accusation. If you discuss the criticism or rejection, try to stay out of the emotional aspects and focus on the truth and the solution.

If someone says they will not use your services due to your inexperience, gaining experience may be the only way to avoid this criticism. In this case, be patient. Each year your experience will grow and that form of rejection will diminish.

Some people will say that they don't want to work with friends. Perhaps in the past they lost a valued friendship over a business disagreement. Don't let them lose a friendship over lack of business this time. Continue your friendship genuinely. They may be more comfortable working with a friend on their next transaction, and they may send you a referral in the meantime.

If you lose out on a listing presentation, you can always ask the seller why they chose another agent over you. Do not be accusatory. You may want to say, "You picked a great agent, but can you tell me what I could have done better to be the agent you choose next time?" Listen to what they tell you and *don't argue with them*. Thank them for their input and learn from it.

If you hear the same type of criticism repeatedly, take a close look at how you are handling your clients and customers. Ask your broker or a trusted friend if there is merit in the client's rejection. Be open to hearing the honest answer and be prepared to change. Don't say, "That's who I am; take it or leave it." If too many people are leaving you and working with others, it may be that part of your technique needs adjustment.

When you are making cold calls, or even calls to people in your sphere of influence, you will receive many "no" answers or "I can't help you" answers. You need to catch someone at just the right moment, a moment when they or someone they know has a need for a real estate agent, so a series of "no" answers is not actually a rejection. Prospecting is a numbers game. The more people you contact, the more chances you have of hearing a positive response. Every "no" you hear is really bringing you closer to a "yes." Count those negative responses as one less negative response, increasing your odds of hearing what you want to hear.

**Essential**

Sometimes you will not know why a client or customer did not choose to work with you and you can only suppose. When you do find out, the answer may be as simple as, "Our kids go to school with her kids." Continue to cultivate your relationships and build your reputation. Next time, it may be you with the stronger connection.

## Be Open-Minded

As a real estate agent you have a great opportunity to meet and interact with a wide variety of people. Although most people will not intentionally express prejudice or judgment, dealing with a person who is far different from you may make you uncomfortable. If the person you are working with has a thick accent, you may have a tougher time understanding him. It is even more important to use your best listening skills in this case. If the person has certain beliefs, maybe those beliefs will appear strange or superstitious to you. Be understanding and accept that not everyone shares the same beliefs you have. Their beliefs are just as valid and important to them as yours are to you.

You may find the requests of some clients and customers odd or confusing. They may refuse to look at a house with a certain address number or in a certain location on the street. These preferences are as real and important to clients as how many bedrooms a house has, and they need to be respected. Spend time learning about other cultures and beliefs and expand your thinking to include the thinking of others. The world is getting smaller, and embracing the multicultural dimensions can be interesting and invigorating.

### Fact

Many people have embraced feng shui, the Chinese art of placement, as a way to stage a home for maximum appeal. Feng shui may have sounded strange to the Western mind a few years ago, but because so many people believe strongly in feng shui and have seen the positive results, it has become more mainstream.

## *Establish a Support Network*

There is plenty of success to go around in the real estate industry, but, unfortunately, not all agents think so. You will encounter agents in your community, and even in your own office, who do not want to help you. They are afraid that if you become successful, it will diminish their success. Even though this isn't necessarily true, such agents might be less likely to befriend you. This can be frustrating when you need someone to give you some insight as to why you failed with a particular client or how you could have better understood a situation.

If you cannot find enough help within the real estate community, find people outside of real estate to assist you. Even if you are surrounded by helpful real estate agents, seeking help outside of real estate will give you a different perspective. It is important to have several people that you can bounce ideas off of—those who can see the areas where you may need to improve and can point you in the right direction.

Cultivate relationships with a group of people from businesses other than real estate to whom you can turn if you need an outside perspective—perhaps an insurance agent (a business with a similar pressure level but not in competition with real estate), or a car salesperson (with the high pressure to perform daily), and other professionals who work with people every day. It is great to have someone give you a different perspective on a situation and to pick you up when you are down.

As you get together with your group, you will find that you can give them new ideas as well. Even if you are a new agent, you still have life experiences to share. Helping one another will strengthen all of you as you pursue your respective careers.

## Negotiation Skills

Understanding people is the first step in being a good negotiator. You will not use these skills so much in getting someone to buy a house, because you are connecting them to a property and letting them make the final decision. You will often need negotiation skills in order to get a contract together.

Once you have written a contract for your buyer, gather all the pertinent backup information to show why your contract is valid. What comparables did you use to come up with the price? Why did you ask for such a high dollar amount in repairs? When you present the offer, be sure to present why your offer was written the way it was written.

### Essential

You will only have a moment to determine the personality styles of the sellers when you are presenting your offer. Are they all about the bottom line or does emotion play a huge part? Which one is the decision-maker? Do they give you clues as you present, to make you change how you present your offer?

When you meet the sellers, start with a positive phrase, such as a compliment about their house or the fact that they graciously took time from their day to meet with you. Be courteous and remember that you are a guest in their home as you present your offer. Do not be confrontational if they bring up unpleasant objections. Instead, make note of their feedback and thank them for their input.

If you think that the sellers are "numbers people," show them the comparables you used and explain why you believe their house is of similar value. If their style is emotional, a little background information about your buyers can help the sellers feel connected to them. You might say, "My buyers think this bonus room will be great, because they are expecting their second child."

## E Alert

If the price of the house concerns the buyer, break it down into manageable segments. "At the current interest rate, this increased price is actually only one hundred dollars a month, just over three dollars a day. That's the cost of a latte. Are you willing to make the small sacrifice of your daily coffee run to get this wonderful house?"

Do not criticize the sellers' house. While it may seem an obvious and easy error to avoid, you may be surprised how easy it is to do. Words such as, "my buyers will need to remodel this kitchen so they deducted the cost of the remodel from their offering price" will not work as well as, "we used this comparable because it has a kitchen similar to yours." Similarly, most sellers do not want to hear that your buyers can't afford more than what they offered. In their mind, that buyer is saying, "I can't afford the house, so just give it to me."

Negotiating on behalf of your seller is equally important and should be handled with the same level of respect and tact. You should use your own set of backup materials and show the buyer why there is value in the property you are selling. Remember that the buyers are making what is likely the biggest investment of their lives. They may have fears and concerns. As you discover what their fears are, you will be better able to negotiate with them.

Keep your negotiations simple. If the buyers bring you an offer with lots of contingencies, let them have whatever contingencies they want, but simplify it by making them all come due at the same time. If the seller wants his closing costs covered by the buyer, ask the seller to add it to his final counteroffer price instead. This will allow the buyers to wrap those costs into their loan and it won't change the seller's bottom line.

**E**ssential

Don't try to overnegotiate. If your seller is willing to sell for a lower price or your buyer is willing to pay more, let it be. You should surely counsel them if you think the decision is unwise, but ultimately you must follow their wishes.

## Have Fun

The real estate business is never boring. You can get on an emotional roller coaster if you allow yourself to, flying high one day and being in the dumps the next. This is great during the highs, but the lows can take a toll. The constant ups and downs can be trying as well. Keep your life in balance so that your emotions do not get in the way of your success. Spend time with your family away from the office and devote special periods to taking care of yourself and your health. Pursue your hobbies and your spiritual practice, and get to know all the people you work with on a personal level. When you enjoy the people you work with, you will enjoy the job and the little setbacks will not bother you as much. When you care for your health and emotional well-being and your life is in balance, the ups and downs of the business will not translate to ups and downs in your personal life.

## Take Care of Your Clients

As an agent you have a great responsibility to take care of your clients and customers as they pursue the American Dream. Homeownership and creating wealth through owning property is the objective.

You can make the process exciting and wonderful for them if you are enjoying life and real estate is simply an extension of your happiness. Imagine helping a young couple buy their first home, especially if the process is tough and you are the one who pulls it through for them. Imagine helping a widow sell her home and move to a smaller place, counseling her as she lets go of the emotional ties and moves on to something easier to take care of alone. The satisfaction you will receive from a job well done is not just seen in the referrals and repeat business that come your way but in the way that people respect you and in the way that you respect yourself.

## Getting Personal

A good real estate agent gets to know her clients and customers on a personal level. She learns what they like and don't like. If it is a couple or a family, she sees the interaction between them. She learns how they act under pressure and how they handle things when they are pleased. She knows their financial history, if they have good credit or bad, and how much money they make. In order to help them be more comfortable in sharing about themselves, she probably relates her own life stories back to them as well. Sharing in this personal way can create very strong bonds between the agent and her clients. These bonds go beyond business, beyond agent and client, and extend into the bonds of true and lasting friendships. Many agents will tell you that their deepest and closest friendships started out as real estate transactions. When you care about someone at this level and when you know someone this well, you will be able to serve their needs better. Your deeper relationships with your clients and customers will enrich all of your lives and will be a part of what creates the road to both personal and financial success for you and those whose lives you touch.

Appendix A

# Suggested Inventory for Vacation Rentals

**A well-equipped vacation** rental will garner happy clients, repeat customers, and referrals. The list that follows will help you and your clients prepare a rental that meets expected standards and helps maintain the property.

1. Entry
   - ☑ Outside mat
   - ☑ Inside rug
   - ☑ Coat closet or coat rack
   - ☑ Full-length mirror (optional)

2. Living Room
   - ☑ One hide-a-bed sofa with two sets of sheets, two blankets, and two pillows
   - ☑ If room is large, an additional sofa instead of a hide-a-bed
   - ☑ One coffee table
   - ☑ Two end tables
   - ☑ Two chairs
   - ☑ Two table lamps
   - ☑ One fireplace tool set and grate
   - ☑ Metal bucket for ashes
   - ☑ Rug in front of fireplace
   - ☑ Artwork or wall hangings
   - ☑ Bookshelves or cabinet with assorted paperback books, children's books, games, and puzzles
   - ☑ Television

- ☑ VCR and/or DVD player
- ☑ Simple stereo with tuner, tape, and CD players, and speakers
- ☑ Decorative items such as baskets, silk plants, or simple statues

**3.** Dining Room
- ☑ Table and chairs to accommodate the number of people the house sleeps
- ☑ Light fixture over table
- ☑ Two sets of placemats for each person
- ☑ Artwork

**4.** Bedrooms
- ☑ King bed, queen bed, or two twin beds per room
- ☑ One bedspread, comforter, or quilt per bed
- ☑ At least two blankets for each bed
- ☑ One or two pillows for each person the bed sleeps
- ☑ Two sets of sheets for each bed (plain white suggested)
- ☑ Pillow shams and dust ruffles for each bed
- ☑ One dresser per bedroom
- ☑ Two nightstands per bedroom or one nightstand between twin beds
- ☑ One lamp per nightstand
- ☑ One alarm clock or clock radio per bedroom
- ☑ One mirror per bedroom
- ☑ Coat hangers
- ☑ Artwork
- ☑ Television in master bedroom with VCR and/or DVD player
- ☑ Chair, if space allows
- ☑ Wall decorations

5. Bathrooms
   - ☑ One mirror
   - ☑ At least 2 sets of towels (bath, hand, washcloth) for each person the house sleeps (plain white suggested)
   - ☑ Towel racks and toilet paper holders
   - ☑ Supply of toilet tissue
   - ☑ At least 2 bath mats per bathroom
   - ☑ Nonslip mat for inside of tub
   - ☑ Washable rug in front of each sink
   - ☑ Toilet brush with holder
   - ☑ Plunger
   - ☑ Wastebasket
   - ☑ Soap dish
   - ☑ Shower caddy for shampoos, etc.
   - ☑ At least one built-in blow dryer
   - ☑ Glass doors or washable shower curtain

6. Kitchen
   - ☑ Refrigerator (with icemaker or ice trays)
   - ☑ Stove with self-cleaning oven
   - ☑ Microwave oven
   - ☑ Dishwasher
   - ☑ Trashcan
   - ☑ Matching set of dinnerware for the number of people the house sleeps, with spares
   - ☑ Matching set of flatware for the number of people the house sleeps, with spares
   - ☑ Set of steak knives, with spares
   - ☑ Matching glassware for three times the number of people the house sleeps
   - ☑ Matching set of plastic cups for the number of twin beds, more if the rental has a pool or deck
   - ☑ Matching wineglasses
   - ☑ Coffee mugs
   - ☑ Coffeemaker and filters
   - ☑ Teakettle

- ☑ Toaster
- ☑ Electric hand mixer
- ☑ One blender
- ☑ At least two frying pans with lids
- ☑ At least four different-sized pots with lids
- ☑ One stockpot
- ☑ Two casserole dishes with lids
- ☑ One slow-cooker
- ☑ Two serving bowls
- ☑ One salad bowl with salad service
- ☑ A set of mixing bowls of various sizes
- ☑ One half-gallon pitcher
- ☑ Two baking sheets
- ☑ Two baking pans
- ☑ Two muffin tins
- ☑ Measuring cups
- ☑ Measuring spoons
- ☑ One broiling pan
- ☑ One set of plastic food storage containers
- ☑ One can opener
- ☑ One bottle opener
- ☑ One corkscrew
- ☑ One potato peeler
- ☑ One colander
- ☑ Set of knives with scissors in block
- ☑ Kitchen tools including stirring spoons, spatula, rubber scraper, tongs, wire whisk
- ☑ Set of wooden spoons
- ☑ Two cutting boards
- ☑ Cheese grater
- ☑ Hot pads, oven mitts, potholders, kitchen towels, cloths, and sponges
- ☑ Mop, broom, dustpan
- ☑ All-purpose spray cleaner
- ☑ Paper towel holder
- ☑ Supply of paper towels and napkins

- ☑ Dish soap and dishwasher soap
- ☑ Dish drainer rack
- ☑ Washable rug in front of sink
- ☑ Kitchen art, if wall space
- ☑ Telephone, phone books
- ☑ Chalkboard with chalk
- ☑ Notepads, pens, and pencils
- ☑ Fire extinguisher
- ☑ Flashlight
- ☑ Candles
- ☑ Matches

**7.** Deck
- ☑ Barbecue grill
- ☑ Barbecue tools
- ☑ Deck table and chairs
- ☑ Table umbrella
- ☑ Lounge chair

**8.** Laundry Room
- ☑ Washer and dryer
- ☑ Laundry soap
- ☑ Iron and ironing board
- ☑ Vacuum cleaner with spare bags
- ☑ Assorted replacement light bulbs

**9.** Optional Items
- ☑ Pool table
- ☑ Hot tub
- ☑ Ski racks
- ☑ Sleds
- ☑ Beach toys
- ☑ Other toys
- ☑ Framed map of the area
- ☑ Specific, typed directions for use of appliances

- ☑ Specific, typed directions for use of stereo, TV, VCR, DVD
- ☑ Menus from local restaurants
- ☑ Typed list of contact numbers for property manager and emergencies
- ☑ List of local grocery stores, post office, pharmacies, banks, movie theaters
- ☑ Selection of recent issues of magazines (usually free at grocery and convenience stores)

Appendix B

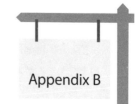

# Internet Resources

**The Internet is** an incredibly rich source for information on just about everything, and the real estate industry has a particularly strong Internet presence. A simple search request offers instant results that a seasoned or budding real estate agent can use to locate nearly any necessity, from schools, licensing information, and industry regulations, to property listings, information on market trends, and promotional products and services.

## *Tackling the Resources*

Today's real estate professionals rely heavily on the Internet. If you are new to the Web, don't be intimidated. It's rather simple to use and you'll find that your search skills develop rapidly.

There are myriad industries that exist to support real estate professionals and virtually all of them have an Internet presence. Of course, the IRS is the definitive voice on tax law, but there are thousands of coaching programs, real estate schools, and Web hosting resources. As the Internet is always growing, there is simply no way to list them all here. The following sites are well established and suggested as a starting point. Happy surfing!

### *Real Estate Schools, State Commissions, and General Information*

**Internet Search Engines:** *www.google.com* or *www.yahoo.com*

Search for general real estate information, find real estate schools in your area (type real estate schools + your area), and locate your state's real estate commission (type real estate commission + your area).

**The National Association of Realtors® public Web site:** *www.realtor.com*

Find lots of real estate information, along with current listings that are a part of the Multiple Listing Service (MLS).

**The National Association of Realtors® Web site:** *www.realtor.org*

Read the Realtor Code of Ethics. Research special designations. Members can access the most current rules about the National Do Not Call Registry.

## *Ethics, Rules, Taxes, and Laws for Real Estate Professionals*

**U.S. Department of Housing and Urban Development Web site:** *www.hud.gov*

Discrimination laws can be violated in subtle ways. To be sure that you are not acting in a discriminatory manner, learn more on the HUD Web site.

**The National Association of Realtors® Web site for RESPA information:** *www.realtor.org/RESPA*

**U.S. Dept. of Housing and Urban Development site, RESPA section:** *www.hud.gov/offices/hsg/sfh/res/respa_hm.cfm*

The Real Estate Settlement Procedures Act (RESPA) designates how a lender or title company can provide benefit to real estate agents. In general, you may not accept contributions or gifts from title companies or lenders, but the rules are complicated and ever-changing. Noncompliance can lead you into trouble. Learn more about RESPA.

**Internal Revenue Service Web site:** *www.irs.gov*

Self-employment tax is the employer and employee shares that are due to the Social Security system and Medicare. Because most real estate professionals are self-employed, they must pay both shares. This cost is currently 15.3 percent but may change annually. Check the IRS Web site for the most up-to-date information. The site is also an excellent source of up-to-date guidelines regarding who is and is not considered an independent contractor.

## *Professional and Personal Development*

**Service Corps of Retired Executives (SCORE):** ✎*www.score.org*

SCORE is a nonprofit with more than 10,500 volunteers, who provide free, confidential small business advice. The volunteers are working and retired business owners, executives, and corporate leaders. SCORE is a resource partner with the U.S. Small Business Administration.

## *Coaching Programs*

There are many programs available. This is a partial, alphabetical list.

**Anthony Robbins**
✎*www.anthonyrobbins.com*

**Buffini and Company**
✎*www.brianbuffini.com*

**Howard Brinton**
✎*www.howardbrinton.com*

**Mike Ferry**
✎*www.mikeferry.com*

**Nightingale-Conant**
✎*www.nightingale.com*

**Steven Covey**
✎*www.franklincovey.com*

**Tom Hopkins International**
✎*www.tomhopkins.com*

**Walter Frey**
✎*www.waltfrey.com*

**Walter Sanford**
✎*www.waltersanford.com*

## Your Personal Web Presence

**The Internet Corporation for Assigned Names and Numbers (ICANN)**

*www.icann.org*

A nonprofit corporation that coordinates several Internet functions. One of its responsibilities is to oversee the domain name system.

**Network Solutions**

*www.networksolutions.com*

This is a good place to start your search for available domain names. If you wish, the company can register your chosen domain name for you, and it also offers many types of Web site hosting packages. Network Solutions has been around for a long time and has a helpful Learning Center. There are now many companies that provide these services. Some specifically serve the real estate industry, providing Web hosting, real estate Web design, and other solutions for the real estate industry.

**Search engine optimization**

*www.submitexpress.com*

*www.website-submission.com*

Search engine optimization is an ever-changing topic and there are hundreds of Web sites devoted to teaching you the best methods to promote your domain. The majority of these sites charge a fee, but you can get a feel for what they sell and what they offer by checking those listed here or by typing "search engine optimization" into your browser and scrolling through the results.

**Overture's word tool**

*http://inventory.overture.com/d/searchinventory/suggestion*

There are several Web sites that allow you to see how many times a word has recently been searched on its system. The information can help you determine which words to attach to your site as meta titles, tags, and keywords to help drive traffic to your site. You'll find Overture's word tool at the address listed here.

## *Marketing and Promotion*

**IPIX Corporation**

*www.ipix.com*

Fisheye lenses are used to take panoramic photographs to produce virtual tours. They can be expensive and they are not available for every camera. The manufacturer of this technology is iPix. Visit their site to determine if the system is the best choice for your needs. See *www.ipix.com/realestate.html* for a page devoted specifically to real estate.

**The National Association of Exclusive Buyer Agents (NAEBA)**

*www.naeba.info*

A site for prospective and current agent members. NAEBA is one of the educational organizations that firms can affiliate with to promote their buyer agency business. The NAEBA also offers an educational Web site for buyers at *www.naeba.org*.

## *Real Estate Franchises*

This is a partial, alphabetical list of real estate franchises and their Web sites. If you are looking for a franchise that is not included on this list, type the name of the franchise into your search engine to be directed to their site.

**Century 21**

*www.century21.com*

**Coldwell Banker**

*www.coldwellbanker.com*

**Help-u-Sell**

*www.helpusell.com*

**Keller Williams**

*www.kw.com*

**Realty Executives**

*www.realtyexecutives.com*

**Realty World**

*www.realtyworld.com*

**RE/MAX**

*www.remax.com*

**Prudential**

*www.prudentialrealestate.com*

**United Country**

*www.unitedcountry.com*

## *Home Warranty Sites: Home Protection Plans*

**American Home Shield**

*www.ahswarranty.com*

**First American Home Warranty**

*www.homewarranty.firstam.com*

**Old Republic**

*www.orhp.com*

Appendix C

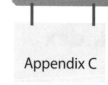

# Phone Numbers for Real Estate Commissions by State

**Alabama:** 334-242-5544
**Alaska:** 907-269-8160
**Arizona:** 602-468-1414
**Arkansas:** 501-683-8010
**California, Northern:** 916-227-0864
**California, Southern:** 213-576-6982
**Colorado:** 303-894-2166
**Connecticut:** 860-713-6150
**Delaware:** 302-739-6150
**District of Columbia:** 202-442-4320
**Florida:** 407-245-0800
**Georgia:** 404-656-3916
**Hawaii:** 808-586-2643
**Idaho:** 208-334-3285
**Illinois:** 217-785-9300
**Indiana:** 317-232-2980
**Iowa:** 515-281-7393
**Kansas:** 785-296-3411
**Kentucky:** 502-425-4273
**Louisiana:** 225-765-0191
**Maine:** 207-624-8603
**Maryland:** 410-230-6200
**Massachusetts:** 617-727-2373
**Michigan:** 517-241-9288
**Minnesota:** 615-296-4026
**Mississippi:** 601-932-9191
**Missouri:** 573-751-2628
**Montana:** 406-444-2961
**Nebraska:** 402-471-2004
**Nevada, Northern:** 775-687-4280
**Nevada, Southern:** 702-486-4033
**New Hampshire:** 603-271-2701
**New Jersey:** 609-292-8280
**New Mexico:** 1-800-801-7505
**New York:** 518-473-2728
**North Carolina:** 919-875-3700
**North Dakota:** 701-328-9749
**Ohio:** 614-466-4100
**Oklahoma:** 405-521-3387
**Oregon:** 503-378-4170
**Pennsylvania:** 717-783-3658
**Rhode Island:** 401-222-2255
**South Carolina:** 803-896-4400
**South Dakota:** 605-773-3600
**Tennessee:** 615-741-2273
**Texas:** 512-465-3900
**Utah:** 801-530-6747
**Vermont:** 802-828-3228
**Virginia:** 804-367-8526
**Washington:** 360-664-6500
**West Virginia:** 304-558-3555
**Wisconsin:** 608-266-5511
**Wyoming:** 307-777-7141

# Index

## N



## O



## P



## R



## S

# The Everything® Career Guide Serie

## Helpful handbooks written by experts.

Trade Paperback
ISBN: 1-59337-583-2
$14.95 ($19.95 CAN)

Trade Paperback
ISBN: 1-59337-432-1
$14.95 ($19.95 CAN)

Trade Paperback
ISBN: 1-59337-433-X
$14.95 ($19.95 CAN)


Available wherever books are sold.
Or call us at 1-800-289-0963 or visit *www.adamsmedia.com*.